ENGLISH *Alive*

Level 2

Barry Scholes and Gill Atha

Collins Educational

An imprint of HarperCollinsPublishers

Notes for the teacher

Book Two consists of fifteen thematic units, each of four pages. The units cover reading, writing and word skills. The accompanying *Teacher's Resource Book* features a variety of photocopiable masters which extend and complement these skills, and are designed to suit the ability range found in most classrooms.

Certain masters have been designated SKILLMASTERS. Each Skillmaster provides a clear explanation and graded practice for a specific skill. It may be kept by the pupil as a permanent reference sheet. Skillmasters are especially useful where a child has a specific difficulty. Those from Level 2 may be used to reinforce later levels of *English Alive*, or indeed any English scheme. The Skillmasters from Level 1 will be helpful where revision practice is required.

Wherever a Level 2 Skillmaster is available this is indicated in Book Two by a reference number e.g. 2.1a. This refers to Activity Master 2.1a in the Teacher's Resource Book, where all support material is grouped under its unit number.

Also included in the *Teacher's Resource Book* are specially written group prediction stories, ideas for the development of speaking skills, and Assessment Masters designed for use at the end of Book Two to test progress.

Level 2 is completed by an audio cassette which provides for a carefully structured development of listening skills.

Acknowledgements

The authors and publishers would like to thank the following for permission to reproduce copyright material:
Angus & Robertson (UK) for extract from 'A Song of Wind' from *Bush Verses* by Will Lawson, reprinted by permission; Blackie & Son Ltd. for extract from *The Willerbys and the Bank Robbers* by Pamela Oldfield; Jonathan Cape Ltd. for extracts from *Tale of a One-Way Street* and *A Necklace of Raindrops* by Joan Aiken, *The Giraffe and the Pelly and Me* and *Danny, the Champion of the World* by Roald Dahl and 'Kidnapped' from *A Light in the Attic* by Shel Silverstein; Century Hutchinson for extracts from *Maggie Gumption* by Margaret Stuart Barry; Collins Publishers for extract from 'My Party' from *Rabbiting On* by Kit Wright, copyright 1978; Andre Deutsch Ltd. for extracts from *The Battle of Bubble and Squeak* by Philippa Pearce and *The Hermit and the Bear* by John Yeoman; Faber for extract from *The Emma Dilemma* by Catherine Sefton; Victor Gollancz Ltd. for extract from *The Sheep-Pig* by Dick King-Smith; Karla Kuskin for 'The Balloon' from *In the Middle of the Trees*, copyright 1958 by Karla Kuskin. Reprinted by permission of the author. Oxford University Press for extracts from *Gone to the Dogs* by John Rowe Townsend, copyright 1984 and *Ghosts, Witches and Things Like That* by Roderick Hunt, copyright 1984, by permission. Penguin Books Ltd. for extract from *The Shrinking of Treehorn* by Florence Parry Heide (Penguin Books, 1975), copyright Florence Parry Heide, 1971; Marian Reiner for 'Witch Goes Shopping' from *See My Lovely Poison Ivy* by Lilian Moore, copyright 1975. All rights reserved. Reprinted by permission. James Simmons and The Gallery Press, Dublin for 'Birthday Poem' from *Poems 1956-1986*, copyright 1986.

The authors and publishers thank the following for illustrations and the use of photographs:
Nancy Bryce, Dorothy Hamilton and Ann Rodger.
British Film Institute (p. 41); Fortean Picture Library (p. 49); F.J. Jarvie (pp. 22 & 51); Photo Library International (p. 61); ROSPA Media Services and Picture Library (p. 18); Scottish Ethnological Archive (p. 50).

ISBN 0 00 314346 5

© CollinsEducational 1991
First published in 1989 by Holmes McDougall Ltd
Published in 1991 by CollinsEducational, 77–85 Fulham Palace Road, London W6 8JB
Reprinted 1992 (twice), 1993 (twice)

Printed in Great Britain by Scotprint Ltd, Musselburgh

Contents

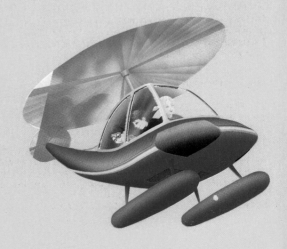

UNIT 1

It was on the second day of Peter's holiday with his grandmother that the Martian came to the cottage. There was a knock at the door and when he went to open it there was this small green person with webbed feet and eyes on the end of stumpy antennae who said, perfectly politely, 'I wonder if I might bother you for the loan of a spanner?'

'Sure,' said Peter. 'I'll ask my gran.'

Gran was in the back garden, it being a nice sunny day. Peter said, 'There's a Martian at the door who'd like to borrow a spanner.'

Gran looked at him over her knitting. 'Is there, dear? Have a look in grandad's toolbox, there should be one there.'

That's not what your grandmother would have said? No, nor mine either but Peter's gran was an unusual lady.

(From *Uninvited Ghosts* by Penelope Lively.)

1 Do you think Peter and his grandmother were surprised to find a Martian knocking at the door? How do you know?
2 What do you think your grandmother would have said?
3 Why do you think the Martian needed a spanner?
4 What do you think antennae are?
5 What do you think will happen next?

Reading for clues

We have already found that Peter's grandmother is rather unusual. Here are some more sentences about her. Think out for yourself what the missing words are. Read the sentences carefully and look for clues. Copy the passage in your book, putting one word for each space.

Peter's gran was an unusual lady, as you will discover. Grandad had died a few years earlier and she ____1____ alone in this isolated cottage in the country, growing ____2____ and keeping chickens, and Peter liked going to stay ____3____ her more than almost anything he could think of. ____4____ was not like most people. She was unflappable and ____5____ you might call open-minded, which accounts for everything that ____6____ next.

(From *Uninvited Ghosts* by Penelope Lively.)

Word study

Each of these sentences has a *Martian* word in it.
Read all the sentences and work out what the Martian word means.

a) The Martian could see a ZONG at the end of the lane.
b) ZONGS keep people warm and dry.
c) A ZONG has doors and windows.
d) People live in ZONGS.

Did you work out that a ZONG is a house or a cottage?
Now see if you can work out the meaning of more Martian words.

1a) People eat BOPPLES.
 b) A BOPPLE has a tail.
 c) BOPPLES live in water.
 d) BOPPLES have fins.

2a) A FLOBLOB is a living thing.
 b) FLOBLOBS grow very tall.
 c) FLOBLOBS never move about.
 d) Birds build nests in FLOBLOBS.

3a) A BOBO has four legs and a tail.
 b) People keep BOBOS as pets.
 c) BOBOS often catch mice.
 d) BOBOS make a mewing sound.

4a) A FLOOSH has wings.
 b) A FLOOSH does not make nests.
 c) A FLOOSH is very big.
 d) A FLOOSH carries people.

Here are four more Martian words. Decide on a meaning for each one and write four
sentences about it. See if your friend can work out what the words mean.

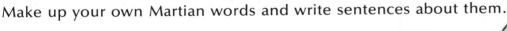

| SPODGE | ZUMZUM | WOOZ | TAPPLEZAK |

Make up your own Martian words and write sentences about them.

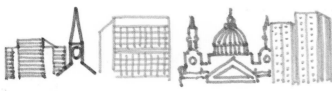

Group names

What name would Peter give to these groups?

1 starling, swan, ostrich, wren
2 spring, summer, autumn, winter
3 guitar, drum, flute, violin
4 carrots, meat, biscuits, bread

5 coffee, cocoa, tea, lemonade
6 grandmother, aunt, uncle, cousin
7 football, netball, tennis, hockey
8 India, Canada, Kenya, New Zealand

Writing

Suppose a friendly Martian called Quogg knocks
on your classroom door. Write a story about
what happens next.

Describe what he looks like, what your teacher
does when he walks in and how you and your
class enjoy having him in your school.

Helping Quogg

Quogg, the Martian, has never seen a bicycle before. Look at this diagram. Tell Quogg what the different parts are used for. Begin like this:

1   The handlebars are for steering the bike.

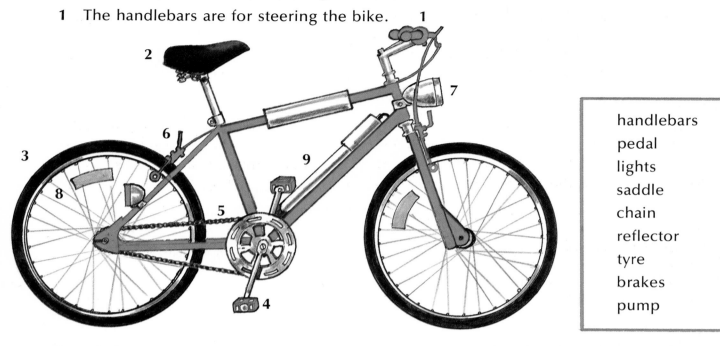

handlebars
pedal
lights
saddle
chain
reflector
tyre
brakes
pump

Descriptions

Quogg is writing descriptions of everything he sees, but he is getting tired and needs your help. These are the last items on his list:

| a car | a dog | a netball post | a pelican crossing | your teacher |

Choose *two* and write a careful description for each one.

Sport

Explain to Quogg the rules of your favourite sport.

Sentences

Quogg's report about Earth contains some very poor sentences. Some of them do not make sense at all! Pick out all the *incomplete* sentences and make them into good sentences.

1   Earth people live in houses.
2   Children go to school
3   Many people own
4   Football is a popular sport.
5   In their gardens they

6   They sleep in
7   At school they
8   Shops are where
9   Many of the Earth people have gardens
10 Earth people are very friendly.

2.1a

To talk about
1 Quogg has room in his flying saucer for ten small objects. Make a list of the things he could take back to help the Martians understand about life on Earth.
2 Imagine you are Quogg and have never been in a classroom before. Walk about and describe all the things you can see. Begin like this:
   "There are lots of very strange creatures in this room. . ."
3 What do you think Quogg would think of our food, the games we play, our pets etc.?

Activities
1 Write and draw about the Martians. Tell what kind of homes they live in, what clothes they wear and the food they eat. What kind of money do you think they use? Collect all your ideas and those of your classmates and make a class book entitled *Life on Mars*.
2 Make a model of the Martian spacecraft. Design a control panel for it.

Outer Space crossword
Copy this crossword into your book.
Then fill in the missing words
using the clues to help you.

Clues across
1 Life form on another planet.
3 Space men wear one.

Clues down
2 Twinkle, twinkle.
4 Earth is one.
6 Three, two, one . . .
8 Unidentified flying object.
10 The centre of the solar system.

Writing
Imagine you are invited for a ride in Quogg's flying saucer.
  Describe what the saucer is like and tell the story of your trip to Mars.

UNIT 2

There were two of them.

Emma was sitting on the bed, and Emma was standing by the door. The Emma on the bed was transparent, and flickery round the edges, but she was undoubtedly *an* Emma, looking exactly the same as the first one.

Emma goggled at her.

'Where have you been?' asked Emma on the bed.

'Oh, gosh!' said Emma by the door.

There couldn't be *two* of her. It was impossible. But there was the Other Emma, sitting smiling on the bed, looking real, except that Emma could see the bed-post through her, and the curtains, and the wardrobe.

'I can . . . I can see through you!' Emma stuttered.

'Can you?' said Emma on the bed. She lifted up her hand and held it in front of her face, gravely inspecting it. 'I *can't* see through me,' she said.

Emma could see through the hand to the face, and right through the face to the yellow curtains on the window.

'I'm glad I can't see through me,' said the Emma on the bed. 'It would be a very yucky feeling, being able to see through yourself, wouldn't it?'

'Yes,' said Emma, confirming by a quick glance that she was solid.

'Are you sure you can see through me?' asked Emma on the bed, sounding not very pleased. 'I look quite normal to me.'

'Yes, I can. I certainly can! I can see the curtains through you.'

(From *The Emma Dilemma* by Catherine Sefton.)

Read these sentences about the passage. Are they true, false or doesn't the passage say? Write *True, False* or *Doesn't Say* for your answers.

1 The two Emmas were alike.
2 Both Emmas had red hair.
3 The Emma on the bed could not see through her own hand.
4 The Emma by the door could see the curtains through the other Emma.
5 The curtains were closed.
6 The wardrobe was next to the door.
7 The real Emma was the one on the bed.

Writing
Imagine you walked into your bedroom and found another you who does all sorts of naughty things to get you into trouble. What happens, and how do   solve your problem?

8

Word study
Using clues
Read this passage carefully, looking for clues. Think out for yourself what the missing words are. Copy the passage into your book, putting one word for each space.

'I've decided I don't like this dream,' said Emma _____1_____ the bed. 'I've never had a dream like this _____2_____. You're not behaving properly, for a person in a _____3_____.'

'If it is a dream,' said Emma, feeling very _____4_____.

'It must be a dream!' Emma on the bed _____5_____ firmly. 'I know, because I can see two of _____6_____ I mean, of us! You look *exactly* like me. _____7_____ can't be two of me, so it *must* be _____8_____ dream.'

They stopped and looked at each other, thinking _____9_____ it.

(From *The Emma Dilemma* by Catherine Sefton.)

Words which sound the same
These words sound alike, but mean different things. Which is the right word?

1 James _____ a stone _____ the window.   (through/threw)
2 Do you _____ with your _____ hand?   (write/right)
3 Paula _____ her mother had bought a _____ dress.   (knew/new)
4 The _____ and white flag fluttered when the wind _____.   (blew/blue)
5 They left _____ coats over _____ by the tree.   (there/their)
6 _____ you like some logs of _____ for your fire?   (would/wood)
7 _____ tomorrow I will have enough money to _____ it.   (buy/by)
8 Can you _____ that ship far out at _____?   (see/sea)

Words which go together
Look at these pictures and find eight pairs. Write them in your book. Begin like this:

1   cup and saucer

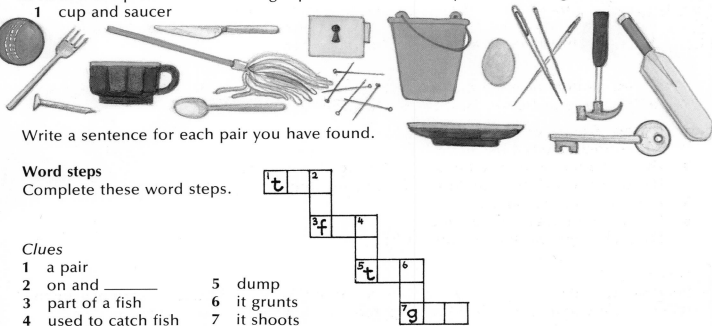

Write a sentence for each pair you have found.

Word steps
Complete these word steps.

Clues

1   a pair
2   on and _____
3   part of a fish
4   used to catch fish
5   dump
6   it grunts
7   it shoots

9

Alphabetical Order

Words in a dictionary are in alphabetical order.
When two words begin with the same letter, look at the second letter.

double	doze	doll	down

All these words begin with the same two letters: **do-**.
When words begin with the same two letters we look at the third letter.
The dictionary order for these words is:

doll	double	down	doze

Put these words in dictionary order.

1 double   down   dock   doze   dot   doll
2 mirror   middle   mix   mill   mist   mind
3 face   far   favourite fall   fan   fail
4 curtain   cuddle   cub   cup   curve   curry
5 gum   guard   guy   gun   guest   guide

In an encyclopedia, or an index, some words begin with a capital letter. Capital letters make no difference to alphabetical order.

Gandhi, ginger, Greece, Greenland, grid are all in correct alphabetical order.

Write these words in the order they would appear in an encyclopedia.

1 Mersey   mouth   Mars   metal   Manchester   Mozart
2 rum   Russia   Rumania   rune   rust   rupee
3 Essex   escort   Eskimo   espionage   Esau   estate
4 Victoria   virus   viking   vixen   violin   Vienna
5 Canada   Cambridge cavalier   cabbage   calypso   Carlisle

Look at these lists of words. In each list *two* words are out of order.
Put the words into correct order.

1	2	3	4	5
pasture	label	Italy	Shakespeare	Africa
palm	ladder	Iceland	Singapore	Albania
piece	lazy	island	Sidney	Alaska
pet	lamp	India	Scott	Austria
plum	lark	itch	Spain	Australia
purple	lance	ivory	Stirling	Aztec

When? How? What? Why? Where?

Questions

1 Make up a question for each of these question words.
Remember: questions begin with a capital letter and end with a question mark.
2 Write five questions you would like to ask a friend in your class. Exchange questions and answer them.
3 Have you ever wanted to meet a famous person? Say who it is, and write ten questions you would like to ask.

2.2b

To talk about

> **I Did a Bad Thing Once**
> I did a bad thing once.
> I took this money from my mother's purse
> For bubble gum.
> What made it worse,
> She bought me some
> For being good, while I'd been vice versa
> So to speak — that made it even worser.
> Allan Ahlberg

1 What do you think 'while I'd been vice versa so to speak' means?
2 How do you think the poet felt when his mother bought him the gum for being good?
3 What rewards does your Mum give you for good behaviour?
4 What does she do when you are naughty?

Writing

Have you ever been praised for something you did not deserve? Or blamed for something you did not do?
Write about it, saying what you did and how you felt.

A poem for you to write
Everyone has some good habits and some bad habits. Your Mum or Dad probably point them out to you all the time.
   Here is an outline for a poem about you and your habits. Think about the things you do and complete each line. Remember poems do not need to rhyme.

Habits
My worst habit is ....
It ....
I also ....
And ....
My good habits are ....
And ....
I'm trying ....
And ....

Tidy your room!
Wipe your feet!
Don't answer back!

11

UNIT 3 Spellbound

1 Haggis the witch was in a furious temper. She had looked everywhere for her tin-opener. It wasn't surprising that she couldn't find it. Her kitchen was the untidiest, filthiest place you have ever seen. There were piles of dirty plates stacked all over the floor, grimy washing was pegged to huge cobwebs that hung from the ceiling, and the cupboards groaned with her horrible home-made jams and pickles — rats-bane relish, bats-blood chutney and jackal-tooth jam.

2 'Someone must have taken it!' she cried, kicking over a pile of unwashed cauldrons. 'Oh well, I suppose I'll just have to magic another one!'

3 Thumbing through an old recipe book, she chanted out all sorts of spells and magic rhymes. Soon the kitchen was full of toys, tin whistles, tiddlywinks and other things beginning with 'T', but she just couldn't get the spell for tin-openers right. She was in a terrible tantrum.

(From *Maggie Gumption* by Margaret Stuart Barry.)

1 Why do you think Haggis could not find her tin-opener?
2 What effect did her spell have?
3 What other things might this spell have made?
4 Read the first paragraph again. Which of these is the main idea?
   a) Haggis was a witch.
   b) All her cupboards were full.
   c) Haggis couldn't find her tin-opener.
5 For each of the following write the paragraph number (*1, 2 or 3*) which tells us about these things.
   a) spells and rhymes
   b) jams and pickles
   c) dirty cauldrons
   d) dirty washing
   e) tiddlywinks

To talk and write about
1 Make up the spells and rhymes which Haggis might have chanted.
2 Make a list of the things Haggis could have made with a 'B' spell.
3 Haggis was in a 'terrible tantrum'. Can you think of any other expressions which have words beginning with the same letter? Here are some to start you off:

| wicked witch | busy bee | piles of pretty plates. |

Adjectives

Read this description of a witch's castle.

> The castle was the home of a witch. It stood at the top of a hill. Its towers rose high above its walls. A path led up to its gate.

It's not a very interesting description is it? Look what happens if we add some adjectives (describing words):

> The old castle was the home of a cruel witch. It stood at the top of a rocky hill. Its five dark towers rose high above its crumbling walls. A steep, twisty path led up to its gloomy gate.

The adjectives have made the description much more exciting. Write each adjective in your book, and next to it write the noun (naming word) it describes.
   Begin like this: old castle, cruel witch, . . .

Rewrite this description of the witch's kitchen. Think of a good adjective to go with each of the underlined naming words.

> In a corner stood a cupboard, its shelves full of bottles and jars. Grizelda, the witch, took down a jar and ran a finger across the page of a book. She gave a laugh and began to stir the mixture in her cauldron. As she chanted words, she was watched by a cat sitting near the fire.

Go on with the story. Tell about the spell she is making and what evil things she does with it.

Spells

ANCIENT SPELLS
contents
1. Invisible spells
2. Flying spells
3. Shrinking spells
4. Growing spells
5. Changing spells
6. Wishing spells
7. Spells to make sensible people do silly things.

CHAPTER 1

Choose *one* of these spells.
Write a recipe for it, and the magic words to make it work.
Write a story about what happens when you use it.

Witch Goes Shopping

Witch rides off
Upon her broom
Finds a space
To park it.
Takes a shiny shopping cart
Into the supermarket.
Smacks her lips and reads
The list of things she needs:
  'Six bats' wings
  Worms in brine
  Ears of toads
  Eight or nine.
  Slugs and bugs
  Snake skins dried
  Buzzards' innards
  Pickled, fried.'

Witch takes herself
From shelf to shelf
Cackling all the while.
Up and down and up and down and
In and out each aisle.
Out come cans and cartons
Tumbling to the floor.
'This,' says Witch, now all a-twitch
'Is a crazy store.
I CAN'T FIND A SINGLE THING
I am looking for!'

Lilian Moore

Read these sentences about the poem. Are they true, false or doesn't the poem say?
Write *True*, *False* or *Doesn't Say* for your answers.

1 The witch expected to find the things on her list.
2 She came into the supermarket on her broomstick.
3 She wanted at least eight toads' ears.
4 She laughed to herself as she went from shelf to shelf.
5 The supermarket manager was angry when she knocked down his cans.
6 She was right in saying the supermarket was a crazy store.
7 She went to another supermarket instead.

Writing
Suppose you were shopping in the supermarket when the witch arrived to do her shopping.
Describe what she did, and what the manager said to her. What did she do then?

Alphabetical order
When words begin with the same three letters we look at the **fourth** letter.
Put these words into alphabetical order.

1 book	boot	boost	boon	boom
2 witch	wither	witness	within	witty
3 spell	speed	spend	spectre	spear
4 castle	cash	case	casual	casserole
5 exclamation	exchange	excuse	except	excited

Supermarkets

1 Find these things in the picture of the supermarket: trolley,   basket,   shelves, special offer,   cold cabinet,   cash register,   check-out.
2 Write a sentence saying what each one is.
3 Look at the signs in the supermarket. Write each one as a heading, and list *five* things you would find for sale there.

Exclamations

Exclamation marks are used whenever someone has an important message:

They are used to give warnings:

Or orders:

They are used when something is exciting:

Or when something hurts:

Write an exclamation sentence for each of these uses.

Activities

1 Make a poster warning people of danger.
2 Make a special offer poster for *one* of the items on the witch's shopping list.
3 Design a label for another item on her list.

15

UNIT 4

'What do you have to do in "Snap"?' asked the Bear.

'You mean what is the object of the game,' said the Hermit. 'Well, the object of the game is to win all the cards by shouting "Snap" . . .'

'Snap!' shouted the Bear, and snatched the pack of cards from the astonished Hermit's hands. 'Like that?' he asked.

'No,' said the Hermit faintly. 'I hadn't finished explaining. There are, in fact, a few more rules. Look, let us have a practice game.' And he took the cards back from the Bear.

'This is called "dealing",' he explained, as he gave out the cards from the pack, laying each one face down on the table. 'You see, I give one to you and then one to me, and then another to you and then . . . please don't turn them all over.'

The Bear did as he was asked.

'Now,' continued the Hermit. 'I collect my cards together into one neat pile with their backs upwards. You do the same.'

The Bear awkwardly scooped up his cards between his paws, bending several of them in half. They stuck out in all directions and the Hermit could even see what some of them were.

'You are supposed to hold them so that their faces don't show,' the Hermit pointed out patiently.

So the Bear clutched them in a pile to his chest. The Hermit could see that the Bear's paws weren't really suitable for holding cards, so he let that do.

'Now, as I was saying before,' he continued, 'the idea of the game is to be ready to shout "Snap" . . .'

'Snap!' shouted the Bear, and dropped all his cards on the ground.

The Hermit was wonderful at keeping his temper. 'We haven't started playing yet,' he pointed out.

'No, I thought we hadn't,' said the Bear, 'but I shouted just to be on the safe side.'

(From *The Hermit and the Bear* by John Yeoman.)

1   Why did the Bear shout "Snap" at the beginning of the game?
2   Why did he say he shouted "Snap" at the end of the passage?
3   Why was the Bear so clumsy at holding the cards?
4   Why do you think the Hermit was trying to teach the Bear to play Snap?
5   Which of these do you think is true about the Bear? Why do you think so?
   a)   he was trying to do as he was told
   b)   he was deliberately trying to annoy the Hermit
   c)   he was being very silly
6   Which of these do you think is true about the Hermit? Why do you think so?
   a)   he was very annoyed with the Bear
   b)   he was very patient with the Bear
   c)   he was wasting his time completely
7   Give the passage a suitable title.

Writing
How would you explain the rules of Snap to the Bear? Write them as clearly as you can.

Reading for clues

Read this passage carefully, looking for clues. Think out for yourself what the missing words are. Copy the passage into your book, putting one word for each space.

The Hermit put his cards down without saying anything ____1____ helped the Bear to pick up his. He then ____2____ them in a neat pile — or as neat a ____3____ as he could manage now that they were all ____4____.

'To make the game more interesting,' said the Hermit, ____5____ a short pause, 'we shall play for acorns. This ____6____ the same as gambling as acorns aren't money. But ____7____ shall be able to count them up at the ____8____ and see who has won the most games.'

(From *The Hermit and the Bear* by John Yeoman.)

Games crossword

Clues across
1 soccer
3 a judge in tennis matches
5 played on a course or links
7 for running on
9 try hard for this one

Clues down
2 for swimming in
4 a game for girls
6 a ball in the net
8 playing frogs
10 also means twenty

Verbs

The word **get** is often over worked.
Rewrite this passage replacing the words **get** and **got** with a better verb (action word). Try not to use the same verb twice.

When Karen got home from school she got her tennis racket. Then she got on her bike and got over to Helen's house. Helen got her racket and a tennis ball and they got playing right away. Helen got the first game, but Karen got the next two. After a while Helen went to get some lemonade. It was a few minutes before she got back.

'I had to get the phone,' she said. 'Your mum says to get home right away. Your dad's just got a new car!'

Begin: When Karen arrived home from school . . .

To talk and write about
1 What do you think will happen next?
2 What has the child forgotten to do?
3 Make a list of places which are dangerous to play in.
4 Design posters to warn of these dangers.

Two into One
Use **and** or **but** to join these sentences. Remember to use **but** when the action in the second sentence is unexpected.

1 The man wound up the clock. It started to work.
2 My dad bought a brand new car. It broke down.
3 Coco the clown did his tricks. Nobody laughed.
4 I forgot my homework. I got into trouble.
5 I was going to score a goal. I tripped and fell.
6 The Hermit decided to teach the Bear Snap.
   He did not have much success.

Sometimes we can join sentences without using **and** or **but**.
Look at these two sentences:

> The children sat on the grass. They played with their toys.

We can join them in this way:

> The children sat on the grass playing with their toys.

We miss out **They** in the second sentence and change play**ed** to play**ing**.

Now join these in the same way.
1 He went down the garden path. He looked for the ball.
2 I stood under the tree. I waited for my friends to arrive.
3 The dog ran down the street. It chased the cat.
4 He sat down after the match. He felt very tired.
5 She worked in the garden. She pulled out all the weeds.
6 He searched through the telephone directory. He looked for her number.

Add words to make these into good sentences.
1 I watched the workmen . . . .
2 The policeman walked down the street . . . .
3 Kelly sat at the table . . . .
4 The boy hurt his leg . . . .
5 The children were busy . . . .
6 He stood at the gate . . . .

1 SPOOKY TOWERS

Your spine-tingling mission is to visit Spooky Towers, find a mysterious box and escape without being frightened to death! An adventure for the BBC range of computers. Ages 7-9.

2 CHECKPOINT

An exciting car rally and quiz game. Drive your car around the board, avoiding hazards if you can. At each checkpoint select your subject from a range of questions. For ages 8 and over.

4 SPELLBOUND

For BBC computers. Trapped in the witch's castle, your only hope is to find three magic words, but watch out for Grizelda and her cauldron of boiling oil! Ages 8-11.

5 PIRATE'S TREASURE

Search for the treasure of Dead-eye Dan, the pirate. Keep your wits about you and watch out for traps! A BBC computer adventure. Ages 8-11.

3 SNAP!

The ever-popular card game as played by the Hermit and the Bear. Snap the Bear before he snaps you! Ages 5 and over.

6 SUPERMARKET

Shop around the superstore collecting all the items on your shopping list. First to the check out with a full trolley is the winner. Ages 8 and over.

1 Look at these games. Which of them:

a) is about a haunted house?
b) is for children aged five and over?
c) is about shopping?
d) is a computer program for ages 7-9?
e) is about a witch's castle?
f) is a card game?
g) do you need to keep your wits about you for?
h) has boiling oil?
i) is also a quiz?

2 Write the names of two games:

a) in which you try to escape,
b) which are race games,
c) a seven year old would enjoy,
d) you would like to play. Say why.

3 Choose a game which all the children in each group below will enjoy. Don't forget to suit each game to the ages of the children. You may use each game only once. The first one has been done for you.

a) Emma, 7 Paul, 8 Rakesh, 9
Emma loves ghosts. Paul hates board games.

> They would all enjoy *Spooky Towers*.

b) Michael, 10 Karen, 8 James, 9
Karen like board games. James likes cars.

c) Jahanara, 8 Sofie, 8 Adam, 8
The girls like magic. Adam likes any computer game.

d) Sara, 6 Sharon, 8 Nicholas, 11
Sara hates board games.

e) Chris, 8 Joanne, 9 Glen, 8
Joanne and Chris like computer games, but Glen doesn't.

f) Alan, 10 Sue, 9 Ranjit, 11
They all like computer games.

To talk about

1 Which games do you like best, those you play alone or those you play with other people? Why do you think this is?
2 Boys spend more time playing than girls do. Do you think this is true? How will you find out?
3 Find out which are the most popular sports in your class and show them on a pictogram.

UNIT 5   FESTIVALS OF LIGHT

Light plays an important part in many religious festivals and special occasions. It is seen to represent Goodness, Truth and Freedom, and is thought to drive away Evil and Fear. Here are some of the many festivals of light from around the world.

Divali is a special festival of light celebrated by Hindus and Sikhs. During Divali fireworks are set off and special little *diva* lamps are lit.

Christians usually celebrate the time of *Advent* which comes just before Christmas. Often a special Advent Wreath is made and one candle a week is lit in the four weeks leading up to Christmas.

Hannukah is a festival celebrated by the Jews. The festival lasts eight days and on each day a candle is lit in a special candle-holder called a *menorah*.

In Sweden another festival of light takes place on December 13th — *St. Lucia's Day*. In this celebration a young girl gets up very early and, wearing a crown of green leaves and candles, she takes special biscuits and coffee to the rest of her family.

1   What does light represent in these festivals?
2   What is the name of the Hindu and Sikh's festival of light?
3   Which special lamps are lit for this festival?
4   When is Advent?
5   On what date is St. Lucia's Day?
6   In which country is this festival celebrated?
7   What is a menorah? Draw a picture of one.
8   How long does the festival of Hannukah last?
9   If you could take part in one of these festivals which would you choose? Say why you prefer that one.

To talk about

1 Describe your favourite festival of light.
2 Which festivals or celebrations do you know which use special lights? Christmas tree lights are one example.

Word study

Opposites

The opposite of light is dark.
Look carefully at these sentences. Replace the underlined words with their opposites.

e.g. The room was very light.
      The room was very dark.

1 He was a very evil man.
2 I did all my sums right today.
3 The clown looked very happy.

4 The old man walked into the park.
5 The fat cat tried to get over the fence.
6 I walked down the winding road.

2.5a

Words with different meanings

Sometimes a word can have two different meanings.

Joan switched on the light.
The leaves were so light the wind blew them away.

In the first sentence light means something to shine in the dark.
In the second sentence light means not heavy.

What do the underlined words mean in each of these sentences?
Use your dictionary to help you.

1 You have to beat the eggs to make a good cake.
2 'I can beat you at running,' the boy said.
3 The soldier was driving the tank.
4 The children filled the tank with water and then put in the fish.
5 A mine is where coal comes from.
6 Hey! That coat is mine.
7 Mum put some clean sheets on my bed today.
8 The teacher cut up some sheets of paper.

Making new words

Often we can make describing words from naming words.

sun (naming word)   makes   sunny (describing word)
shine (naming word)   makes   shiny (describing word)

Make describing words from these words.

fun   thirst   wood   gold   soap   rain

Write a sentence for each describing word you have made.

Writing sentences

Finish each sentence in any way you wish.
Then add another sentence to go with it.

1 When I switched on the light . . . . . .
2 I found a very small . . . . . .
3 Daniel was walking down the street when . . . . .

4 The giant shouted . . . . . .
5 The lady wore a green hat which . . . .
6 I am afraid of . . . . . .

My party

My parents said I could have a party
And that's just what I did.

Dad said, 'Who had you thought of inviting?'
I told him. He said, 'Well, you'd better start writing,'
And that's just what I did.

To:

Phyllis Willis, Horace Morris,
Nancy, Clancy, Bert and Gert Sturt,
Dick and Mick and Nick Crick,
Ron, Don, John,
Dolly, Molly, Polly —
Neil Peel —
And my dear old friend, Dave Dirt.

I wrote, 'Come along, I'm having a party,'
And that's just what they did.
Kit Wright

1   Write in alphabetical order the first names
    of the girls who were invited to the party.
2   Make a similar list for the boys.

A birthday poem
(for Rachael)

For every year of life we light
a candle on your cake
to mark the simple sort of progress
anyone can make,
and then, to test your nerve or give
a proper view of death,
you're asked to blow each light, each year,
out with your own breath.
James Simmons

1   Why does the poet say we light candles on a
    birthday cake?
2   Why does he say we blow them out?
3   Say which of the poems you like best and why.

How old is the child in the picture?
How do you know?

Writing
Read *My Party* again. Pretend you have been invited to the party. Write a letter in reply to your invitation.
Write a story about the party, saying what games you played and what food you had to eat.

Making sentences using 'because'
Read this sentence.

> Lisa cannot go to the party.

Why can't she go? We could say:

> Lisa cannot go to the party, **because she is ill.**
>
> or Lisa cannot go to the party, **because she has not been invited.**

We use **because** to tell us why she can't go.

Use **because** to join these sentences.
1   I fell off my bike. I was not holding on with both hands.
2   We do not come to school on Saturday. It is the weekend.
3   The old lady was very grateful. I helped to carry her shopping.
4   I am afraid of dogs. One bit me when I was very young.
5   We had to stay inside. It was raining very heavily.

Reading clues
Sometimes when we read there are words we don't know or don't understand. Yet if we read carefully we often find clues to help us.

Do you know what **illuminated** means?
Read this sentence carefully.

> When we switched on the light, the whole room was **illuminated.**

Do you think illuminated means: **a)** in darkness *or* **b)** lit up?
Of course now we can guess that illuminated means **lit up.**

Read these sentences carefully and choose which meaning goes with the word in heavy type.

1   During a **famine** many families starve and die.
    a)   a time of little food   **b)**   a holiday
2   The aeroplane was carefully towed out of its **hangar.**
    a)   runway   **b)**   shed
3   The priest talked to the **congregation** about Jesus.
    a)   school children   **b)**   people in church
4   John cracked the shell of the walnut and ate the **kernel.**
    a)   the stalk   **b)**   the middle of the nut
5   After the cricket match the players went into the **pavilion** for refreshments.
    a)   a hut   **b)**   a castle

Finding out
1   Use your class or school library to find pictures showing the festivals of light you have learned about.
2   Find out and write about Christian celebrations.
3   Look again at the photograph of the menorah on page 20. Find out what *Shalom* means.

UNIT 6 Time

When I was nine I came to an arrangement with a grandfather clock; it was disastrous. Never trust a clock. Believe me — I know. I'll tell you about it.

I was in the hall of our house, all by myself. Except for the clock. I'd just come in from school. The clock said ten past four. And I said, out loud, because I was fed up and cross as two sticks, 'I'd give anything to have this afternoon all over again.'

'Would you now,' said a voice. 'That's interesting.'

There was no one there. I swear. Mum was out shopping and my brother Brian was off playing with his mate down the road. The voice came from the clock. I looked it in the eye and it looked back, the way they do. Well, they've got faces, haven't they? Faces look.

'I deal in time, as it happens,' the clock went on. 'Had some bad time, have you?'

Funny stuff, time. I mean, it can be good or bad, and you're always being told not to lose it and we all spend it and some of us kill it. You can have overtime and half-time and summer time and the time of your life. And there's always next time. And my time's my own, so's yours.

I nodded.

'Sometimes,' said the clock, 'I can lend a hand.' It twitched one, from eleven minutes past four to twelve minutes past. 'Tell me all, then.'

(From *Uninvited Ghosts* by Penelope Lively.)

Read these sentences about the story. Are they true, false or can't you be sure? Write *True, False* or *Can't be sure* for your answers.

1   The story begins when the boy was ten years old.
2   He was the only person in the house.
3   The grandfather clock was in the hall.
4   School finished at half past three.
5   The boy was very cross.
6   Brian was playing on his bike.
7   Brian was his younger brother.
8   The boy wanted to have his morning all over again.

Reading for clues

Read the passage carefully, looking for clues. Think for yourself what the missing words are. Write one word for each space.

So I told. About how at dinner I was ____1____ a bad mood because of having a fight ____2____ Brian and when Mum kept going on at me ____3____ something I kept thinking 'Oh, shut up!' only unfortunately ____4____ was meant to be a think got said out ____5____ accidentally so then Mum was in a very bad ____6____ indeed with me and I got no pudding. And ____7____ on the way back to school Brian and I ____8____ another fight and my new pencil case got kicked ____9____ a puddle and all dirtied over. And we were ____10____ and Mrs Harris told us off.
(From *Uninvited Ghosts* by Penelope Lively.)

To think and talk about

1   What do you think will happen next?
2   What makes you think so?
3   Have you ever wanted to have time all over again? Why? What would you do?
4   Do you think the boy in the story wants to enjoy things all over again, or to make them happen differently? What makes you think so?

Word study

Look again at the story. It has lots of expressions about time in it.
Here are some of them:

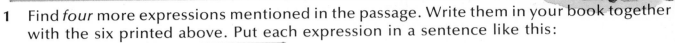

| good time | bad time | losing time |
| killing time | spending time | next time |

1 Find *four* more expressions mentioned in the passage. Write them in your book together with the six printed above. Put each expression in a sentence like this:

> I had a good time at the party.

2 Can you think of any more time sayings? Make a collection of them. Here are some to start you off.

| timetable | pastime | Old Father Time |

3 What do you think 'as cross as two sticks' means?
Complete these well known similes (comparisons). Use each one in a sentence.

| coal | ice | gold | iron | snail | grass | kitten | feather |

1 As green as _____
2 As slow as a _____
3 As cold as _____
4 As good as _____

5 As light as a _____
6 As black as _____
7 As hard as _____
8 As soft as a _____

Time line

Carefully re-read the story and the passage with the missing words. Now look at the time line. It shows some of the day's events in the order they happened. Copy the time line into your book and add these other sentences in the correct time order.

| I started to talk to our clock. |
| School ended. |
| Fought with Brian again. |
| Had my dinner. |
| My pencil case fell into a puddle. |

12.00 — Had a fight with Brian.

— Said 'Shut up' and Mum heard me.

— Told off by Mrs Harris for being late.

3.30
4.10 — Arrived home from school.
4.12

Making sentences

Here are the first and last sentences of some three-sentence stories. Copy them into your book, making up your own middle sentence for each one. Use the word bank to help you.

| burglar | caught | arrested | kicked | time | mend | shouted | tired |

1 I was very cross at dinnertime . . . . . . Mum did not give me any pudding.
2 It was nearly ten o'clock. . . . . . . I had to go to bed.
3 The clock was broken. . . . . . . We threw it away.
4 I passed the ball to John. . . . . . . It was a goal.
5 The police arrived. . . . . . . He was put in prison.
6 My dad went fishing. . . . . . . We ate them for tea.

May

S	M	T	W	T	F	S
			1	2	3	4
5	6	7	8	9	10	11
12	13	14	15	16	17	18
19	20	21	22	23	24	25
26	27	28	29	30	31	

Dentist

Look at the calendar and answer these questions.
1 How many days are there in May?
2 How many Sundays are there?
3 How many Wednesdays are there?
4 On what days do these days fall?
   a) 9th   **b)** 14th   **c)** 31st
5 If today is the 10th of May, what day was it yesterday?
   What day will it be tomorrow?
6 Jackie has circled her birthday in blue. What day and date is her birthday?
7 How many days are there between Jackie's birthday and her visit to the dentist?
8 On what day was the 30th April?
9 On what day is the 1st of June?

2.6a ENGLISH ALIVE!

Yesterday
Look at these sentences.

> Today the bus <u>leaves</u> on time.
> Yesterday the bus <u>left</u> on time.

Change these sentences in the same way.
1 Jackie goes to the dentist today. Yesterday Jackie _____ to the dentist.
2 There are four birds on the grass. Yesterday there _____ four birds on the grass.
3 It is a sunny day today. Yesterday it _____ a sunny day.
4 Tom drinks orange juice. Yesterday he _____ orange juice.
5 Tonight I am going to watch a football match. Last night I . . . .
6 He jumps across the stream. Last week . . . .
7 We take some apples. Yesterday . . . .
8 Joanne and Louise play netball this afternoon. Last week . . . .

Word study
Look closely at this word.
| clock |

Can you find in it a word which means a fastening which can only be opened by a key?
| c **lock** — lock |

Now see if you can find these words.
1 The sound a clock makes . . . .   tickled
2 The pointing part of a clock . . . .   shandy
3 The opposite of thin . . . .   grandfather
4 A fruit or seed with a hard shell . . . .   minute
5 Something used to wind a clock . . . .   monkey
6 A word which means to finish . . . .   pendulum
7 The number that comes after seven . . . .   weights
8 The opposite of her . . . .   chime

Joining sentences

Look at these sentences.

> Helen is the girl. She won the race.

They can be joined by using **who.**

> Helen is the girl who won the race.

If we are talking about an animal or a thing we use **which** instead of who.

> I went to help the cat. The cat was stuck up the tree.
> I went to help the cat **which** was stuck up the tree.

Use **who** or **which** to join these sentences.

1   Ravi is the boy. He saved the drowning girl.
2   He took his watch to a watchmaker. The watchmaker mended it.
3   This is my coat. My coat was lost.
4   The boy spoke to the policeman. The policeman told him the time.
5   He reached down the book. The book was on the shelf.
6   This is Mr. Winter. He lives in Edinburgh.
7   She looked after the dog. The dog had broken its leg.
8   I went to see the old lady. She used to be a dinner lady.

Using a dictionary

Write these words in alphabetical order.
Then use a dictionary to find out what they mean.

pendulum	sundial	century	watch	annual

Writing

1   Here is the beginning of a story about a speaking clock. Copy it into your book and then finish it in any way you wish.

> It was my birthday and I was very excited. As soon as I saw the postman coming down our path I ran to greet him. He gave me a bundle of cards and letters and a big box. It was my birthday present from Uncle Toby. He always sends me something really special.
>   I rushed inside and opened the box. It was a red alarm clock.
>   'Huh, that's not very special,' I said in disappointment.
>   'Oh, yes I am,' said a voice which seemed to come from the clock, 'and I'll show you just what I can do!'

2   Write a letter of thanks to Uncle Toby for the clock he sent you.

UNIT 7   The Memory Tree

'My boy, you've got a treasure there. What you have is a leaf from the Memory Tree.'

'What's the Memory Tree?'

'It grows in the forests of Brazil. Have you had any Brazil nuts lately?'

'We did have some,' said Gus.

'A leaf might have got among them. The tree was found once, but then it was lost again. Nobody knows where it grows. Just sometimes, once in a way, a leaf turns up.'

'What does it do?'

'If you hold it scrunched up in your hand, you can remember anything.'

'Anything in the world?'

'Anything in the world.'

'Even if it hasn't happened?'

'Even if it hasn't happened.'

Gus quickly scrunched up the Memory leaf in his hand. The prickles hurt a little, but not too badly.

'Now, say what you want to remember,' said Mr Brown.

'I want to remember how I was given a zebra for my birthday,' said Gus, 'and how I rode it right through the town, crossing all the traffic lights when they were red . . .'

(From *Tale of a One-Way Street* by Joan Aiken.)

1   Who was talking to Gus?
2   What is so special about the leaf?
3   How did Gus come to have the leaf?
4   What did Gus want to dream about?
5   Do you think there really is a Memory Tree? Say why you think so.
6   In one line Mr. Brown says 'It grows in the forests of Brazil', but later he says 'Nobody knows where it grows.' How can both of these be true?

Reading for clues
Think for yourself what the missing words are in this passage.
Write one word for each space.

Right away, that very minute, he could remember his ___1___, and how he had looked out of his window to see the zebra standing tied to the front door-knocker. ___2___ could remember the zebra's name, Horace, and his red ___3___ and bridle, with brass bits, and the way all ___4___ motorists had hooted when Horace galloped across the lights, and ___5___ the police had started after him on their motorbikes ___6___ he had been much too fast for them to ___7___ up.

To think and talk about
1   What do you think will happen next in the story?
2   How do you think Gus felt to have a leaf from the Memory Tree?
3   What is your favourite memory?

Writing
Imagine you found a leaf from the Memory Tree.
Would you choose to remember an exciting thing you once did?
Or would you prefer to remember something that has never happened?
Write about your memory and draw a picture to go with it.

Word study

Read these sentences carefully.

> The Memory Tree was found once, but then the Memory Tree was lost again. Nobody knows where the Memory Tree grows.

Now read these.

> The Memory Tree was found once, but then it was lost again. Nobody knows where it grows.

The second story sounds better because it does not keep saying 'the Memory Tree' over and over again. Instead we use the word 'it'.

Here are some more words we often use to save repeating a noun (naming word).

| he | she | it | him | his | her | they | them | we | us | you |

Use one of these words to replace the words underlined in the sentences below.
1. Have you had any Brazil nuts recently? A leaf might have got among the Brazil nuts.
2. The zebra liked Gus. Gus was good fun.
3. The zebra galloped through the traffic lights. The traffic lights were on red.
4. The lady dropped the shopping bag. All the lady's shopping fell out of the bag. The lady was annoyed.
5. Mr Brown picked up the leaf that Gus had dropped. Mr. Brown gave the leaf back to Gus.
6. My friend and I want to find Gus. My friend and I want to use Gus's leaf. My friend and I will give the leaf back to Gus.

More than One

Words ending in —y.
If a word ends in —y, we usually change the -y to -ies to make it plural.
  memory memories   sky skies

But if the letter before the y is a vowel (a, e, i, o, u) then add an s.
  valley valleys   day days

Change these into more than one.

| turkey | try | tray | boy | journey |
| berry | key | fly | ferry | chimney |

Copy these sentences, changing the words in heavy type to more than one.
1. The **lady** wore clothes made of silk.
2. We went to the zoo to see the **monkey.**
3. There were golden sands and lovely clear water all round the **bay.**
4. The **butterfly** had beautiful wings.
5. The orange **jersey** belonged to my Uncle Paul.

Remembering

Study carefully the picture of Gus on the zebra, and then answer the questions overleaf without looking back.

2.7a

2.7b

29

How well did you remember?
Answer from memory these questions about the picture of Gus on the zebra.

1 How many cars were in the picture?
2 How many policemen were there?
3 What colour was Gus's jumper?
4 What time was it on the church clock?
5 What was the woman in the brown coat holding?
6 What was Gus doing with his hands?

Look at the picture again. Were you correct?

A flow chart
Here are six pictures that show you how to plant a tree.
Think of a sentence for each picture.
Copy the flow chart into your book and put a sentence in each box.

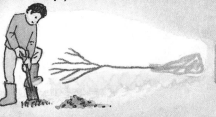

Dig a hole.

Put in a supporting stake.

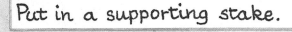

In the right order

These sets of instructions have got mixed up. Write them out correctly in your book.

1 Making toast
Put some butter and marmalade on.
When it is ready take it out.
Put some bread under the grill.

2 Painting a picture
Mix the colours you want.
When you have finished, leave it to dry.
Paint your picture.

3 Going to bed
Get into bed.
Put on your pyjamas.
Brush your teeth.
Take off your clothes.

4 Reading a book
Read the story.
Open the book.
Choose a book.
Put it back on the shelf.

In these sets of instructions an important one has been left out.
Copy out the instructions filling in the missing line.

1 Fishing
Put the bait on the hook.
Put the line in the water.
....
Take the fish home.

2 Washing up
Put washing up liquid in the water.
Wash all the dishes.
Stack them on the draining board.
....
Put them away neatly.

3 Using the telephone
Put your money in the slot.
Lift the receiver.
....
Speak.
Put the receiver down.

4 Watching television
Plug in the television set.
Switch on.
Select the channel.
Watch the programme.
....

A poem for you to learn

The Camel
The camel has a single hump;
The dromedary, two;
Or else the other way around.
I'm never sure. Are you?
Ogden Nash

1 Read the first line of the poem very carefully.
2 Say it over and over again until you can say it without looking at the book.
3 Do the same with the second line.
4 Now say the first and second lines together without looking at the book.
5 Learn the next line and say all three lines together.
6 Learn the last line. Recite the poem you have just learned.

Use your dictionary to find out how many humps a dromedary has.

To talk and write about

Try to think back to when you were very little. What is the earliest thing you can remember? Can you remember your first day at school? Can you remember your first holiday? How old were you?

Choose something that happened as far back as you can remember and write about it, saying what happened.

UNIT 8

At first Ginger saw nothing of particular interest. The television screen did not interest him, nor the sounds that proceeded from the set. There were gun-shots, screams, alarm-bells and sirens: Ginger paid no attention.

But then there was another sound: a little scuffling and scratching and a subdued *Creak!* . . . *Creak!* . . . *Creak!* Nobody looking at the television screen even turned a head: they were used to the fidgetings of Bubble and Squeak by now.

But the ginger ghost in the shadows began to move. From shadow to shadow he slipped, round the back of the chairs and the couch, until he was close to the table.

From inside their cage on the table the gerbils saw him. They froze. Ginger saw them and leapt . . .

The television viewers were aware of something that hurtled through the air, and an impact like an explosion. That was Ginger reaching the cage. Suddenly everyone was shouting or shrieking. The cage skidded off the table and on to the floor with a crash. The whole of the barred side and roof flew off in one piece. The two gerbils leapt for their lives.

(From *The Battle of Bubble and Squeak* by Philippa Pearce.)

Read the story carefully before answering these questions.
1   Read the first paragraph again and then study these titles:
   a)   Nothing Interests Ginger
   b)   The Sleepy Cat
   c)   My Favourite Television Programme
   Which of these titles is most suitable for paragraph 1?
2   Look at paragraph 2. Choose the best of these titles:
   a)   The Family Watch TV.
   b)   The Gerbils Escape
   c)   Ginger Hears the Gerbils
   Say why you made your choice.
3   Do the same for paragraph 3.
   a)   Ginger, the Hunter
   b)   Furniture
   c)   The Ghost That Lived in the House
4   Choose a title for the last paragraph.
   a)   The Flying Cat
   b)   Run, Gerbils Run!
   c)   The Broken Cage
   Say why you made your choice.

5   Look at the last paragraph again and answer these questions.
   a)   What did the cat do?
   b)   What were the people doing at first?
   c)   What did they do after the cat jumped?
   d)   What damage did the cage suffer?
   e)   What did the gerbils do?
6   Did Ginger plan all along to attack the gerbils? How do you know?
7   Think of an exciting title for the story. Say why you have chosen it.

Reading for clues

Think for yourself what the missing words are in this passage.
Write one word for each space.

Peggy saw one gerbil and dived for it and _____1_____ it.

Ginger saw the other gerbil — Bubble — and dived _____2_____ it and caught it.

Peggy was screaming because, holding _____3_____ gerbil, she could do nothing about the other one. Sid _____4_____ yelling because he was trying to frighten Ginger into _____5_____ his prey. Amy was screaming, anyway. But Mrs Sparrow was _____6_____ screaming. She was the only one within reach _____7_____ Ginger and Bubble, and she was inspired. She flung _____8_____ forward on to Ginger's tail, gripped it, held it _____9_____ both hands, hauled on it.

(From *The Battle of Bubble and Squeak* by Philippa Pearce.)

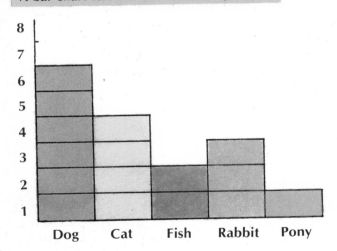

A bar chart to show our favourite pets

Several children were asked to name their favourite pet. Look carefully at this bar chart and say whether the following sentences are true, false or we can't say.

Write *True*, *False* or *Can't Say* for your answers.

1 Six children prefer dogs.
2 More children like fish than rabbits.
3 Ponies are the least popular pets.
4 Nobody likes guinea pigs.
5 Dogs are the most popular pets.
6 Rabbits are preferred by five children.
7 Twenty children took part in the survey.
8 Some children liked more than one pet.

Activities

1 Make a bar chart of your favourite wild animals.
2 Make a pet chart (see sheet **2.8c**) with headings for name, size, colour, food, movement, sounds etc. Make this pet chart as detailed as possible.

Writing

Paragraph building

Complete the second sentence in an exciting way, and then add one or two sentences of your own to make a paragraph.

1 The cage crashed to the floor. The mice ran as . . .
2 Max, the guard dog, was very fierce. The postman was . . .
3 The circus elephant walked slowly round the ring. Suddenly she saw a mouse and . . .
4 I bought two goldfish from the pet shop. When I got home I . . .

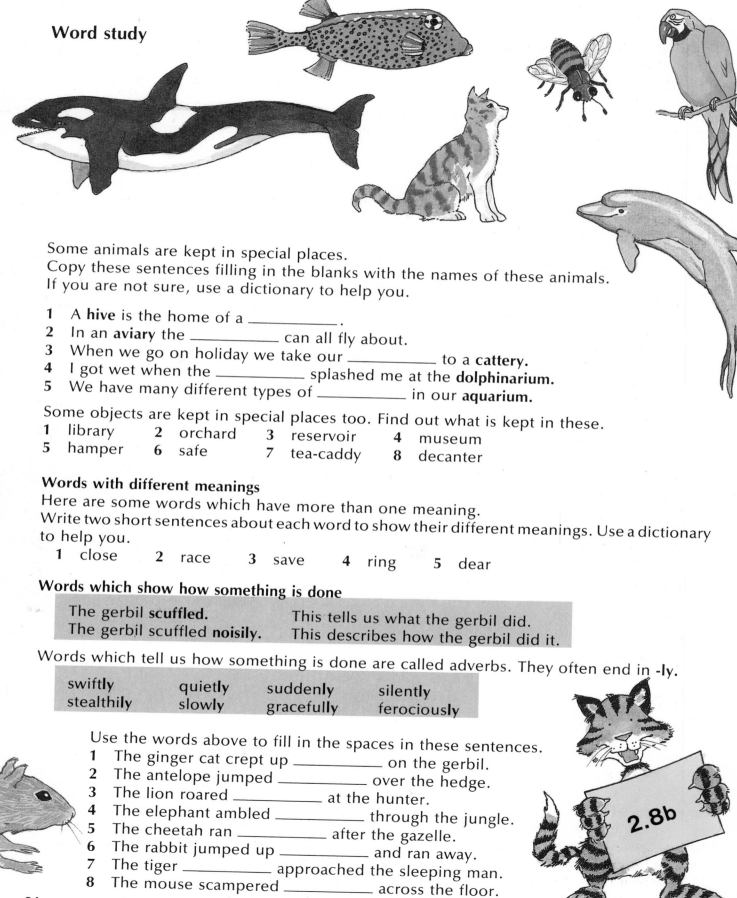

Word study

Some animals are kept in special places.
Copy these sentences filling in the blanks with the names of these animals.
If you are not sure, use a dictionary to help you.

1   A **hive** is the home of a _____ .
2   In an **aviary** the _____ can all fly about.
3   When we go on holiday we take our _____ to a **cattery**.
4   I got wet when the _____ splashed me at the **dolphinarium**.
5   We have many different types of _____ in our **aquarium**.

Some objects are kept in special places too. Find out what is kept in these.

1   library   2   orchard   3   reservoir   4   museum
5   hamper   6   safe   7   tea-caddy   8   decanter

Words with different meanings
Here are some words which have more than one meaning.
Write two short sentences about each word to show their different meanings. Use a dictionary
to help you.

1   close   2   race   3   save   4   ring   5   dear

Words which show how something is done

| The gerbil **scuffled**. | This tells us what the gerbil did. |
| The gerbil scuffled **noisily**. | This describes how the gerbil did it. |

Words which tell us how something is done are called adverbs. They often end in **-ly**.

| swiftly | quietly | suddenly | silently |
| stealthily | slowly | gracefully | ferociously |

Use the words above to fill in the spaces in these sentences.
1   The ginger cat crept up _____ on the gerbil.
2   The antelope jumped _____ over the hedge.
3   The lion roared _____ at the hunter.
4   The elephant ambled _____ through the jungle.
5   The cheetah ran _____ after the gazelle.
6   The rabbit jumped up _____ and ran away.
7   The tiger _____ approached the sleeping man.
8   The mouse scampered _____ across the floor.

2.8b

34

Pets

'Oh, look at those two poor little things in the corner cage!' said Dandy. 'Don't they look sad?'

'They're not at all pretty,' Mrs Sealyham observed. 'Straight hair and small noses.'

'They're not part of my regular stock,' Mr Retriever told them. 'Somebody brought them in. They'd been abandoned, I'm afraid. I said I'd try to find a home for them.'

'That was kind of you,' said Mr Sealyham. 'You must be quite a person-lover.'

'I wouldn't fancy having a *stray!*' sniffed Mrs Sealyham.

'Strays can make very good pets if you catch them young,' said Mr Retriever. 'And you could have these two very cheaply, at a price just enough to cover my costs.'

'*Two* children, when I don't really want *any!*' exclaimed Mrs Sealyham.

'It would be quite a bargain,' said Mr Sealyham thoughtfully. 'Two for the price of one, or even less. But I must say, they're terribly thin!'

'They're perfectly healthy,' said Mr Retriever. 'Just feed them up a bit and you'll be surprised by the difference. But do remember that most dogs overfeed their people. I hate to see fat overfed people waddling along.'

'If we had them,' said Sammy, 'that would be one each.'

'Quite so,' said Mr Sealyham. He added, to his wife, 'It might prevent the pups from squabbling.'

(From *Gone to the Dogs* by John Rowe Townsend.)

1   Who are the Sealyham family? Which clues tell you?
2   Give Mrs. Sealyham's reasons for not having the pets.
3   Give Mr. Sealyham's reasons for wanting them.
4   Think of a good title for the passage.
5   Who do you think the 'pups' are in the last line?
6   Would you like to belong as a pet to a family of animals?
    Give reasons for your answer.

Writing

Pretend you are for sale in a pet shop. Describe the animals who come to look at you, and write a story about what happens when an animal family buys you.

To talk and write about

Make up an imaginary animal to keep as a pet.
Give it a name.

What does it look like?
What does it eat?
Where does it sleep?
What noise does it make?
How does it move?

How does it behave:
a)   when it is hungry?
b)   when it is happy?
c)   when it is angry?
d)   when it is cold?
e)   when it is frightened?
f)   when it is tired?
g)   when strangers come to your house?
h)   in the car?
i)   at the vet's?
j)   when you bring it to school?

UNIT 9   Sky

¹ There was an old man and an old woman, and they lived in a very cold country. One winter day the old man said to the old woman.

² 'My dear, it is so cold, I should like it very much if you would make a good, hot apple pie.'

And the old woman said, 'Yes, my dear, I will make an apple pie.'

³ So she took sugar, and she took spices, and she took apples, and she put them in a pie-dish. Then she took flour, and she took fat, and she took water, and she began to make pastry to cover the pie. First she rubbed the fat into the flour, then she made it into a lump with a little water.

⁴ Then she took a roller and began to roll out the pastry.

While she was doing this, the old man said, 'Look out of the window, my dear, see, it is beginning to snow.'

And the old woman looked out of the window at the snow, coming down so fast out of the white sky.

⁵ Then she went on rolling the pastry. But what do you think happend? A little corner of the sky that she had been looking at got caught in the pastry. And that little bit of sky was pulled under the roller, just the way a shirt is pulled into the wringer. So when the old woman rolled her pastry flat and put it on the pie-dish, there was a piece of sky in it! But the old woman did not know this. She put the pie in the oven, and soon it began to smell very good.

From *A Necklace of Raindrops* by Joan Aiken

Which of these titles do you think is best for the story?

a) The Extraordinary Pie   **b)** A Little Piece of Sky   **c)** Apple Pie for Tea
Say why you think so.

Scanning

When we read for information it is often best to **scan**. We do not read every word, but just **scan** over the text to find the details we are looking for.

Scan the passage to find where the following details are mentioned.

The first one has been done for you.

Details	Which part of the passage (1-5)?
1 The sky was caught in the pastry.	5
2 Rolling out the pastry.	?
3 Where the couple lived.	?
4 The old man looked out of the window.	?
5 It was starting to snow.	?
6 It was winter.	?
7 Mixing the flour and fat.	?
8 She put the apples in a pie-dish.	?
9 The pie was put in the oven.	?

Read the last paragraph again carefully. Complete these sentences with the correct details.

1 The old lady was rolling _____ .
2 A _____ got caught in it.
3 When the pastry was _____ there was a _____ in it.
4 The old woman did not _____ .
5 The pie was put in _____ and it _____ .

This is the recipe the old woman used to make her pie, but it has got all mixed up. Use the story to help you put the instructions in the right order.

Recipe for Apple Pie
1. Sprinkle flour on the table and use a rolling pin to make the pastry smooth and flat.
2. Core and slice the apples.
3. Add the fat and rub the mixture between your fingers.
4. Put the chopped apples in a pie-dish and add spices.
5. Put some flour in the bowl.
6. Add some water and make the pastry into a dough.
7. Put the pie into a hot oven to bake.
8. Put the pastry on pie-dish and trim off any extra.

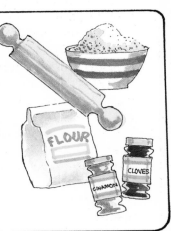

Writing

The pie must be very special with a piece of sky in it. What do you think might happen when the pie is eaten? Write your own ending to the story. Begin like this:

When the pie was ready the old woman carefully cut a piece for her husband. As he started to eat it . . .

Reading for clues

Sometimes a word may have more than one meaning. If you read the sentence carefully you will find a clue to the meaning of the word.
Read these sentences. Decide which meaning is best for the word in heavy type. The first one has been done for you.

A 1) The snow was coming down **fast.**   a) tightly
   2) The corner of the sky was stuck **fast** in the pie. b) quickly

Answer: **A** 1   quickly
      A 2   tightly

B 1) The blacksmith was hard at work in his **forge.** a) workshop
   2) The boy **forged** his parent's signature.   b) copied

C 1) Jason was painting his **model** aeroplane.   a) someone who shows off clothes
   2) The artist's **model** stayed quite still.   b) a small copy of an object
   3) My sister is a **model** in a fashion show.   c) someone who sits so they can
                                                  be drawn

D 1) 'No chewing gum' is one of our school **rules.** a) in charge
   2) **Rule** a straight line.   b) draw
   3) Henry VIII **ruled** our country a long time ago. c) instructions which must be
                                                          followed

The Balloon

I went to the park
And I bought a balloon.
It sailed through the sky
Like a large orange moon.
It bumped and it fluttered
And swam with the clouds.
Small birds flew around it
In high chirping clouds.
It bounced and it balanced
And bowed with the breeze.
It skimmed past the leaves
On the tops of the trees.
And then as the day
Started turning to night
I gave a short jump
And I held the string tight
And home we all sailed
Through the darkening sky,
The orange balloon, the small bird
And I.

Karla Kuskin

Read the poem carefully. Look closely at the words at the end of each line. Some of these words have the same sound. They rhyme.

balloon — moon

Write in your book the words in the poem which rhyme with:

a) sky **b)** breeze **c)** night.

Copy these word balloons. Add more rhyming words for each one.

slow
no
grow

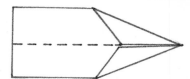

bit
hit
grit

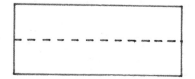

head
red
said

Making a paper aeroplane

Use the instructions at the bottom of the page to make a paper aeroplane. Then try these experiments.

Throw your paper plane. Describe how it flies. How far can it travel? Write the answers in your book. Now try these with your aeroplane.

1   Add a piece of Plasticine or a paperclip to the front of your plane. Does it fly better? Add more weight. What happens now?

2   Try launching the plane pointing downwards, and then again nose upwards. Which makes the plane fly better?

3   Add a rudder to your plane by making flaps at the back of the wings. Bend the flaps up, then down, and then one up, one down. Write down what happens each time.

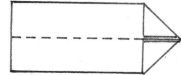

Fold the oblong paper in half and then open out again.

Fold the corners into the middle.

Fold the new corners into the middle.

Writing

Look at these marvellous sweets!

> I can remember especially the Giant Wangdoodles from Australia, every one with a huge ripe red strawberry hidden inside its crispy chocolate crust . . . and the Electric Fizzcocklers that made every hair on your head stand straight up on end as soon as you popped one into your mouth . . . and there were Nishnobblers and Gumglotters and Blue Bubblers and Sherbet Slurpers and Tongue Rakers, and as well as all this, there was a whole lot of splendid stuff from the great Wonka factory itself, for example the famous Willy Wonka Rainbow Drops — suck them and you can spit in seven different colours.
>
> (From *The Giraffe and the Pelly and Me* by Roald Dahl.)

Imagine that a new line of wonderful sweets has just been made at the Wonka factory. They are called **Sky Riders.** All of them are so special they make you able to fly. If you believe in them that is!

Here are some of them.

Sunset Sizzlers	**Super Swoopers**	**Marshmallow Clouds**
Moon Munchers	**Raspberry Rockets**	**Loony Loopers**

The Wonka Factory has asked your teacher to test them out before they go on sale in the shops. She brings them into class and one by one you try them out. What do they taste like? What effect do they have? Describe what happens.

Make up some more varieties of these sweets and test them out. Design wrappers for one or more of these sweets.

Make up your own instructions

Write down, perhaps with drawings to help, your own detailed instructions for making something. When you have finished pass them on to a friend to see if they can be followed.

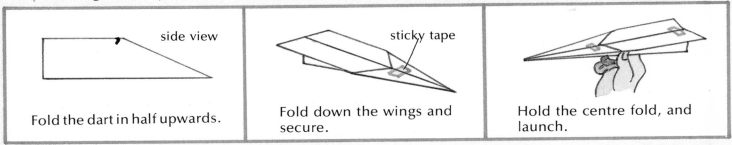

Fold the dart in half upwards.	Fold down the wings and secure.	Hold the centre fold, and launch.

UNIT 10  FEARS

I didn't dare look round to see if they were stopping and coming back after me. I was certain they would stop. Any policeman in the world would stop if he suddenly passed a small boy in a tiny car chugging along a lonely road at half past two in the morning. My only thought was to get away, to escape, to vanish, though heaven knows how I was going to do that. I pressed my foot harder still on the accelerator. Then all at once I saw in my own dim headlamps the tiny gap in the hedge on my left-hand side. There wasn't time to brake or slow down, so I just yanked the wheel hard over and prayed. The little car swerved violently off the road, leaped through the gap, hit the rising ground, bounced high in the air, then skidded round sideways behind the hedge and stopped.

The first thing I did was to switch off all my lights. I am not quite sure what made me do this except that I knew I must hide and I knew that if you are hiding from someone in the dark you don't shine lights all over the place to show where you are. I sat very still in my dark car.

(From *Danny, the Champion of the World* by Roald Dahl.)

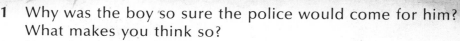

1 Why was the boy so sure the police would come for him? What makes you think so?
2 How do you think the boy was feeling as he hid in the car?

Reading for the main idea

When an author writes a paragraph he usually has one main idea in mind, although he may mention other things too.
In the first paragraph Roald Dahl writes about:
— the police car stopping and beginning to chase Danny,
— Danny's fear of being caught,
— the gap in the hedge.

Read the first paragraph again and decide for yourself which of these three is the main idea of the paragraph.

Now read the second paragraph. Which of these is its main idea?
— switching the lights off,
— hiding from the police,
— sitting still.

Reading for clues
Think for yourself what the missing words are in this passage.
Write one word for each space.

The hedge was a thick one and I couldn't __1__ through it. The car had bounced and skidded sideways __2__ such a way that it was now right off __3__ track. It was behind the hedge and in a __4__ of field. It was facing back towards the filling-station, __5__ in very close to the hedge. I could hear the __6__ car. It had pulled up about fifty yards down the __7__ and now it was backing and turning. The road __8__ far too narrow for it to turn round in __9__ go. Then the roar from the motor got louder and __10__ came back fast with engine revving and headlamps blazing.
(From *Danny, the Champion of the World* by Roald Dahl.)

Writing
Can you think of a reason why the boy was driving the car, and where he might be going?
 Imagine you are Danny and write about your adventures that night. Explain how you escape from the police and what happens next.

To talk about
Read this letter carefully.

Dear Editor,
I am writing to complain about the awful series of horror films that has been shown on television recently. I think that the characters are far too frightening and the things they do are ghastly and dreadful.
 I am also concerned that many young children may be watching these terrible films and having nightmares as a result. If these programmes have to be shown they should be broadcast late at night when young children are safely asleep.
Your sincerely,
Frank N. Stein

Do you agree with this letter? Do you enjoy watching horror films? Are some horror films too frightening? Do you think they should be shown at a later time?
 Write a letter to a newspaper complaining either that you find horror films too frightening, or that they are on too late for you to watch.

Fears

Mrs. Beaton's class have been talking about their greatest fears. Here are their reports. Read them carefully and then copy and complete the bar charts to show the information they give.

Girls' report

There were fourteen members in our group and exactly half of them were frightened of spiders. Two girls did not like horror films and the same number were afraid of going to the dentist. The rest of the group said they were afraid of the dark.

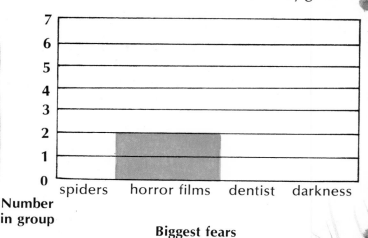

Number in group

Biggest fears

Boys' report

We had fifteen in our group and not one of them was scared of spiders, but John and Ali didn't like snakes. Three boys were scared of going to the dentist and one was scared of being in hospital. Four people were frightened of the dark, which is one less than the number who were frightened by exams.

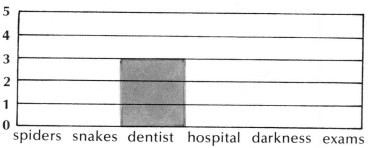

Number in group

Biggest fears

To talk about

Discuss the fears of the children in your class.

Make bar charts to show the results.

Are the boys and girls afraid of the same things? Discuss why this is so.

Can you say why you are afraid?

Does it help to talk about your fears?

Paragraph building

We have said that a paragraph should have one main idea. Write a short paragraph of your own (two or three sentences) about each of these ideas:

1 A fear of dogs
2 A horror film you have seen
3 Running away from trouble
4 Ghosts

Think of a suitable title for each of your paragraphs.

The Silent Spinney
What's that rustling behind me?
Only a cat.
Thank goodness for that,
For I'm afraid of the darkness,
And these tall trees
Are silent and black,
And if ever I get out of here, mate,
I can tell you I'm not coming back.

There's a dark shadow out in the roadway,
See if there's someone behind that tree,
For I'm afraid of the darkness
And it might jump out at me.

My sisters are scared stiff of spiders,
My mother is frightened of mice,
But I'm afraid of the darkness,
I'm not coming this way twice.

Seamus Redmond

1   What causes the rustling noise?
2   How are the trees described in the poem?
3   Who is afraid of mice and spiders?
4   What is the poet afraid of?
5   What do you think a spinney is? Use a dictionary to see if you are right.
6   Do you think *The Silent Spinney* is a good title for the poem? Say why you think so.
7   Think of a different title for the poem.

Word building
1   We can make describing words by adding **-ful** to naming words.
   e.g. fright + ful = frightful
        fear + ful   = fearful

Add **-ful** to these naming words and then put them in sentences of your own.

wonder	dread	fear	sorrow	colour
cheer	help	care	tear	thank

2   Here are two lists of words. Pair them together so that they make longer words.
   e.g. door + step = doorstep

night	**step**
grave	print
day	hole
key	mare
arm	dream
bath	yard
foot	chair
door	room

Now write a sentence for each of the words you have made.

Activities
Write and paint a picture about the worst nightmare you have ever had.

UNIT 11
Writing and PRINTING

Chinese writing

Chinese writing began thousands of years ago. It was first written on a kind of paper made out of linen rags. The writing was done with a bamboo brush dipped in ink.

Chinese writing is very different from our own. The Chinese do not use an alphabet, so their words are not built up from separate letters like ours.

m - a - n = man   w - o - m - a - n = woman

Instead the Chinese have a symbol or character for each word.

亻 = man   亻 = men   女 = woman

This makes learning to write in Chinese very difficult!

Legend says that it was Chang Kit, a minister to one of the Chinese emperors, who invented these picture graphs. He studied the mountains, trees and the water, which are all very important to the Chinese way of life. Chang Kit also looked at the animals, and from his many observations the earliest Chinese words were written as pictures or pictographs.

Here are some original Chinese pictographs and how they have changed over the years.

sun
mountain
tree
horse
moon

Now answer these questions about Chinese writing.

1   How is Chinese writing different from our own?
2   How did the pictographs develop?
3   What is a legend?
4   What other two words are used in the passage which means the same as pictographs?
5   Why do you think that the pictographs have changed over the years?

To talk and think about

1   What problems do you think there would be in making a Chinese dictionary? Try to think of ways of solving this problem.
2   Find some Chinese writing. What do you notice about how the writing is set out? How might this cause difficulties for English-speaking people who want to learn to read Chinese?

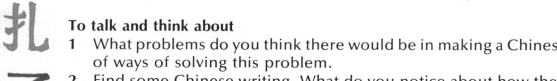

Telegrams

Before most people had telephones the only way they could get in touch with a distant person quickly was to send a telegram. A telegram message was sent from a post office and delivered within an hour or so by a special messenger. Telegrams were expensive because a charge was made for each word. This made people use as few words as possible. A message like the one below would have been very expensive:

> Dear Mum,
> I've forgotten my key, so could you please leave the spare one with Mrs. Mulligan or Mr. Jones?
> Thanks,
> Julie.

Instead, Julie would have shortened it:

> Mum — forgotten key — leave spare with neighbour — Julie.

Can you send this message in seven words or less?

> The car has broken down, and we've got a flat tyre. We won't be arriving until tomorrow evening.

Do the opposite with these. Write two sentences or more to give each message in full.
1 Police — arrested man — bank robbery — freed — innocent.
2 Wembley — football final — Rovers — goal — win — trophy.
3 Delayed — Paris — fog — flying — Edinburgh — tomorrow.
4 Storm — roof damaged — fence down — no one hurt.
5 School — Summer Fair — famine relief fund — £267 raised.

Morse code

Pictographs are really a kind of code. Look at the Morse code printed below. Instead of pictures this code is made up of dots and dashes. It is used by ships and aeroplanes to transmit messages.

Use the code to find out what this message says. Write it in your book.

···/———/··· ··—·/··/—·/· ·—·—·/———/·—·—·—··· ···/····/··/···

·———/———/·—··/··—··/—·—·—· ···/····/···/·—·/·

···/··/·—·/—·—·/··/—·—·/· ··—·/·—·/··/· ··—·/····/—··

——··/·—·/··/·—·—·/·/·—··—·/·/·—·—·/··· ··—·

·—··/··/··—·—·/·· ——··/———/·——·/—·/··· ···/·/·—·/·—·

····/·/·——··/·——· ——·—·/··—·/··/——·—·/·—·—/·—·—·/·—·

1 What has happened to the *Jolly Susan*?
2 Where are the passengers?
3 Is the boat sinking?
4 Who do you think sent the message? What makes you think so?
5 Write a Morse code message back to the *Jolly Susan*.

A	• —	N	— •
B	— • • •	O	— — —
C	— • — •	P	• — — •
D	— • •	Q	— — • —
E	•	R	• — •
F	• • — •	S	• • •
G	— — •	T	—
H	• • • •	U	• • —
I	• •	V	• • • —
J	• — — —	W	• — —
K	— • —	X	— • • —
L	• — • •	Y	— • — —
M	— —	Z	— — • •

Pictographs

Try making your own pictographs.
Think of pictures to replace the words of your message.
Here are some examples.

| I | live | see | in | like/love | can | up | down | one |

Use the pictographs to find out what these sentences say.
Write them in your book.

1

2

Now make up some sentences of your own using pictographs.

Fiction books

Here are some titles of well-known story books. Try to work out what they are. The authors'
names may give you a clue.

1   by Richard Adams

2   by Roald Dahl

3   by Robert Louis Stevenson

4   by Dick King-Smith

If we wanted to find any of these books in a library we would have to look in the fiction
section, because all story books are fiction books.
In the fiction section the books are arranged in alphabetical order of the authors' surnames.
The pictograph titles above would be in this order.
1   *Watership Down* by Richard Adams
2   *The Witches* by Roald Dahl
3   *The Sheep-Pig* by Dick King-Smith
4   *Treasure Island* by Robert Louis Stevenson

Put these fiction books into alphabetical order of the authors' surnames.

Stig of the Dump — Clive King

The Jolly Postman — Allan and Janet Ahlberg

Charlie and the Chocolate Factory — Roald Dahl

A Necklace of Raindrops — Joan Aiken

Dr. Doolittle — Hugh Lofting

The Emma Dilemma — Catherine Sefton

Charlotte's Web — E. B. White

The Borrowers — Mary Norton

Α Β Γ Δ Ε Ζ Η Θ Ι Κ Λ Μ
a b g d e z   th i k l m

Ν Ξ Ο Π Ρ Σ Τ Υ Φ Χ Ψ Ω
n x o p r s   u

Word study

Copy these sentences about writing and printing. Choose a word for each space.

1. Chinese people _____ using pictographs and symbols. (right/write)
2. The Phoenician alphabet is _____ up of twenty-two letters. (maid/made)
3. Egyptian paper, or papyrus, was made from _____. (reeds/reads)
4. We can use _____ writing to send messages. (pitcher/picture)
5. Printing means we can easily have more than _____ copy of a book. (won/one)
6. I wrote a letter using _____ coloured ink. (blue/blew)
7. You have to know the _____ to a code before you can read it. (quay/key)
8. Chinese writing was done on a _____ of paper. (piece/peace)
9. The Morse Code is used by aeroplanes and ships at _____. (sea/see)
10. You can _____ books about writing from a bookshop. (buy/by)

Making opposites by adding -un

Sometimes a new word can be made by adding **un-** to the beginning of a word.
  e.g. usual — unusual

Add **un-** to these words and then put each one in a sentence.

happy	screw	safe	kind
fair	comfortable	lock	tidy

If you are not sure of any word, check it in your dictionary.

Activities

1. Look at all the different alphabets in the pages of this unit. Which are most alike?
2. Write out the English alphabet in your best writing. Can you write the letters backwards?
   e.g. ꟼ Ǝ Ɔ Ԑ A
3. Find out how many languages are spoken by the children or teachers in your school. Make a graph to show the results.

А Б В Г Д Е Ж З И Й К Л М
a b v g d e   z i   k l m

Н О П Р С Т У Ф Х Ц Ч Ш Щ
n o p r s t u f

Chit-Chat

Unit 12

CONTENTS

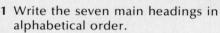

1 Write the seven main headings in alphabetical order.
2 In which two sections are the titles *not* in alphabetical order?
3 Choose seven items you would like to read.
Write them in page number order.
4 Write *two* of these items:
   a) a story suitable for page 20
   b) an article for page 16
   c) an article for Mike Green's column
   d) a review from the News and Reviews section
   e) a poem for the Readers' Poems section.
5 *Either* paint a picture for the painting competition *or* draw and colour a cartoon to go on page 24.

The Smash Street Kids

bookworm

1 What do you think the cartoon characters are saying?
2 What do you think will happen next? Draw more pictures for the story.

Double words

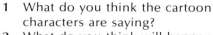

1 Which double words do you think these pictures show?
2 Draw amusing pictures of these words: milk teeth, hot dog, heavy-handed, light-headed, crab-apple.
3 Draw two other pictures using words of your own.

The Ghost of Newby Church

This photograph of the altar of Newby Church in Yorkshire should have been quite ordinary. It was a perfectly ordinary day when it was taken. The vicar had arranged for a series of photographs to be taken of his church. He planned to have them printed as postcards which he could then sell to raise money for the church fund.

The photographer had chosen a sunny day to take the pictures. He had spent time in getting the best views both inside and outside the church. The last few pictures were to be taken of the nineteenth century altar, which is the centre-piece of the church. It has an attractive stained glass window behind it. The vicar hoped it would make one of his best picture postcards.

The camera was set up on its stand and the pictures were taken. Nothing unusual was seen. Perhaps there was a sudden slight chill in the air — a cool draught, perhaps, which blew past and was gone, such as might be felt sometimes in large buildings — but nothing else. The photographer was well pleased with his morning's work.

When the prints were ready and the photographer looked through them, he noticed on one the figure of a monk standing on the altar steps. How could the monk have appeared on the photograph? Could this really be a ghost? If so, how could it have been seen by the camera yet by no one else at the time the picture was taken.

The prints were shown to the vicar, but he too was baffled. He did not think his church was haunted. No one had ever seen the ghostly monk before. What could be the answer to the mystery?

Experts examined the camera and the film. They agreed that this was a genuine photograph. The film had not been touched and the camera wasn't able to take double exposures (this is when two pictures are taken on the same piece of film by mistake).

The answer to the mystery is simple. The photograph was taken by opening the shutter of the camera for a few seconds. This meant that the picture was taken very slowly. So slowly, in fact, that if someone walked across in front of the camera quickly enough, it would not be able to take his photograph, unless he stood still for a moment. And if he happened to be wearing a hooded robe, and had a white sheet over his face . . .

(From *Ghosts, Witches and Things Like That* by Roderick Hunt.)

1 How do you think the vicar felt when he saw the photograph?
2 Why did experts agree that it was a genuine photograph?
3 Who do you think the ghost was? What makes you think so?
4 Explain in your own words how the photograph was taken.

PRIVATE? NO!

Punctuation can make a difference.

Punctuate these notices so that each has a different meaning.

> Private
> No swimming
> Allowed

does not mean the same as

> Private?
> No. Swimming
> Allowed.

Willard R. Espy

> Danger
> No bicycles
> Allowed

> Newtown Police
> Wanted for Murder
>
>
>
> Punk Perkins
> Have you seen this man?
> £500 Reward

> Cycling on this
> land is
> strictly forbidden.
> No ball games

Look into the past

This photograph shows a school in Manchester in 1913.

1. Write two things which are different from schools today.
2. Write two things which are the same as schools today.
3. Would you like to have been at this school in 1913? Say why.

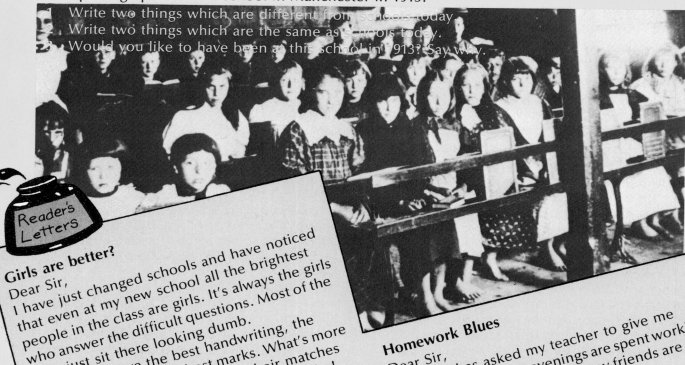

Reader's Letters

Girls are better?

Dear Sir,

I have just changed schools and have noticed that even at my new school all the brightest people in the class are girls. It's always the girls who answer the difficult questions. Most of the boys just sit there looking dumb.

The girls have the best handwriting, the neatest books and the best marks. What's more the netball team win nearly all their matches whilst the football team is a complete joke!

At my last school a girl won first prize in your painting competition. Two of the prizes in your poetry competition were won by girls at my new school. None of the boys has won anything!

Yes, as far as I am concerned, girls are quite simply better than boys.

Yours faithfully,
Anita Choudhury (Hillington)

Homework Blues

Dear Sir,

My mum has asked my teacher to give me homework. Now my evenings are spent working at the kitchen table, when all my friends are out playing. It really makes me angry.

My mum keeps going on about how it is good for me, and my teacher says my classwork is improving, but I've had enough of it.

What do your readers think about homework?

Yours faithfully,
S. Thomas (Newtown)

Editor's note: Come on, boys, you can't let Anita get away with that! Surely you can't be so bad? And what do our girl readers think about it?

Chit-Chat would like to hear your views on these or any other subject. Please write now to **Readers' Letters.**

Kidnapped!

This morning I got kidnapped
By three masked men.
They stopped me on the sidewalk,
And offered me some candy,
And when I wouldn't take it
They grabbed me by the collar,
And pinned my arms behind me,
And shoved me in the backseat
Of this big black limousine and
Tied my hands behind my back
With sharp and rusty wire.
Then they put a blindfold on me
So I couldn't see where they took me,
And plugged up my ears with cotton
So I couldn't hear their voices.
And drove for 20 miles or
At least for 20 minutes, and then
Dragged me from the car down to
Some cold and mouldy basement,
Where they stuck me in a corner
And went off to get the ransom
Leaving one of them to guard me
With a shotgun pointed at me,
Tied up sitting on a stool . . .
That's why I'm late for school!

Shel Silverstein

What an excuse! Did you notice how the poet has used detail to make this fantastic story sound real? Look at the words he uses to describe the car, the wire and the basement. You can almost smell the damp basement and feel the wire cutting into your wrists.

Can you think of an even more unlikely excuse for being late? One that would make your teacher howl with laughter or turn purple with rage? Write it as a poem or a story. Add detail to make it sound real. When you have finished, give it to your teacher and stand well clear!

Readers' Poll

Yes, it's the *Chit-Chat* Readers' Poll time again. These are the things we would like you to tell us about:

1) Yourself, your hobbies and interests.
2) Your favourite *Chit-Chat* features.
3) Your ideas to make *Chit-Chat* even better.

Fill in the special *Chit-Chat* Readers' Poll form (reference **2.12a**), available from your teacher.

UNIT 13   Talking and Listening

When the lady said he could see the Principal, Treehorn went into the Principal's office with his form.

The Principal looked at the form, and then he looked at Treehorn. Then he looked at the form again.

'I can't read this,' said the Principal. 'It looks like SHIRKING. You're not SHIRKING, are you, Treehorn? We can't have any shirkers here, you know. We're a team, and we all have to do our very best.'

'It says SHRINKING,' said Treehorn. 'I'm shrinking.'

'Shrinking, eh?' said the Principal. 'Well, now, I'm very sorry to hear that, Treehorn. You were right to come to me. That's what I'm here for. To guide. Not to punish, but to guide. To guide all the members of my team. To solve all their problems.'

'But I don't have any problems,' said Treehorn, 'I'm just shrinking.'

'Well, I want you to know I'm right here when you need me, Treehorn,' said the Principal, 'and I'm glad I was here to help you. A team is only as good as its coach, eh?'

The Principal stood up. 'Good-bye, Treehorn. If you have any more problems, come straight to me, and I'll help you again. A problem isn't a problem once it's solved, right?'

(From *The Shrinking of Treehorn* by Florence Parry Heide.)

1 What was Treehorn's problem?
2 What did the Principal think Treehorn's problem was? Why did he think so?
3 How do you know that he did not really understand?
4 What did Treehorn say which made the Principal believe the problem was solved?
5 Pretend you are Treehorn. Write a note to the Principal explaining what is happening to you.

To talk about
1 Have you ever had difficulty in getting grown-ups to listen to you? What happened? Why do you think they did not listen?
2 Act out a situation where an adult does not really listen to what you have to say.

Not now . . .

1 Make a list of all the things grown-ups say to you when they are too busy to listen, or when you are pestering them.

Here are some to start you off:

"Yes, that's nice."

"In a few minutes."

"Don't be such a pest!"

"That's lovely. Now go away and play."

2 Emma is looking out of her window when she sees a monster looking at her from across the road. She tries to tell her mother, but she is too busy ironing. This is how the conversation goes:

EMMA: Mummy, there's a monster across the road!
MOTHER: That's nice, dear.
EMMA: Mummy, he's staring at me!
MOTHER: Not now, love, I'm busy.
EMMA: He's crossing the road. He's coming here!

Notice this is written in play form. Copy it into your book. Then continue the conversation as the monster opens the gate, comes up the drive, looks in the window, rings the bell and so on. Perhaps it is a real monster, or perhaps not? Make up your own ending.

When it is finished act it out with a friend.

What are they saying?

Look at this picture. What do you think the people are saying? Write their words in your writing book.

Listening

Babe is a pig who is thought to have savaged a sheep. Fly, his sheepdog friend, is trying to find out what really happened. Babe talks to the sheep all the time, but Fly has never done so, except to bark orders. This is what happens when she tries to talk to them.

'Ba-a-a-abe!' bleated the sheep eagerly.

'What does that mean, bonehead?' barked Fly. 'Was it or wasn't it?'

'Wolf,' said the sheep.

Somehow Fly controlled her anger at the creature's stupidity. I *must* know what happened, she thought. Babe's always talking about being polite to these woolly idiots. I'll have to try it. I must know. She took a deep breath.

'Please . . .' she said. The sheep, which had begun to graze, raised its head sharply and stared at her with an expression of total amazement.

'Say that agai-ai-ai-ain,' it said, and a number of others, overhearing, moved towards the collie.

'Please,' said Fly, swallowing hard, 'could you be kind enough to tell me . . .'

'Hark!' interrupted the first sheep. 'Hark! Ha-a-a-ark!' whereupon the whole flock ran and gathered round. They stood in silence, every eye fixed wonderingly on her, every mouth hanging open. Nincompoops! thought Fly. Just when I wanted to ask one quietly the whole fat-headed lot come round. But I must know. I must know the truth about my Babe, however terrible it is.

'Please,' she said once more in a voice choked with the effort of being humble, 'could you be kind enough to tell me what happened this morning? Did Babe . . .?' but she got no further, for at the mention of the pig's name the whole flock burst out into a great cry of 'Ba-a-a-aabe!'

Listening, for the first time ever, to what the sheep were actually saying, Fly could hear individual voices competing to make themselves heard, in what was nothing less than a hymn of praise. 'Babe ca-a-a-ame!' 'He sa-a-a-aved us!' 'He drove the wolves awa-a-a-ay!' 'He made them pa-a-a-ay!' 'Hip hip hooray! Hip hip hooray! Hip hip hoora-a-a-ay!'

(From *The Sheep-Pig* by Dick King-Smith.)

1 Why was Fly angry?
2 Why did Fly control her anger?
3 Why were the sheep amazed?
4 How do you know that Fly would not have been so polite if the situation had not been so serious?
5 Why do you think the sheep say Babe's name as 'Ba-a-a-abe'?
6 In the last paragraph what is it that Fly does for the first time ever?

In the right order

The sentences below tell what happened when Fly spoke to the sheep, but they are in the wrong order. Put them in the right order.

> She listened to what the sheep were saying.
> At first she was angry with the sheep.
> All the sheep gathered round her in amazement.
> The sheep told her that Babe had saved them from the wolf.
> Then she controlled her anger and spoke to the sheep politely.
> Fly went to the sheep to ask them what had happened.

Group names

We say a flock of sheep, a herd of cattle and a litter of pups.

1 What group name do we give to these?
> bees   football players   singers   sailors   teachers   whales
2 What are these groups of?
> orchestra   forest   fleet   army   bouquet   pack
3 Write three sentences of your own, each containing a different group name.

Boasts

Do you think a man really could be so hungry? Many people make boasts about things that could not possibly be true. Make up boasts about people who are:
   tall, small, fat, thin, mean, miserable, clever, stupid, lazy, rich.
e.g. I know a man who is so tall he climbs a ladder to shave himself.

Here are some ideas for boasts about things.
   a deep hole, an overgrown garden, a very real picture, a house with many rooms,
   a busy street, a fast car.
e.g. We have a hole in our street so deep it has kangaroos at the bottom.

Can you think of any more?
Draw or paint a picture for each one, and put it in a class book of *Boasts*.

UNIT 14 Cops and Robbers

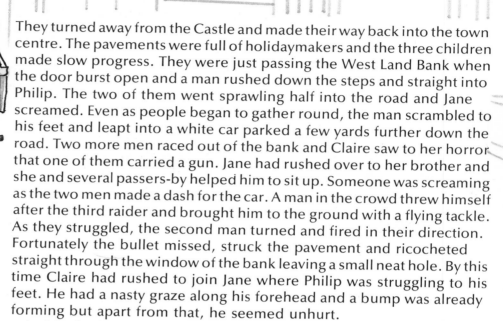

They turned away from the Castle and made their way back into the town centre. The pavements were full of holidaymakers and the three children made slow progress. They were just passing the West Land Bank when the door burst open and a man rushed down the steps and straight into Philip. The two of them went sprawling half into the road and Jane screamed. Even as people began to gather round, the man scrambled to his feet and leapt into a white car parked a few yards further down the road. Two more men raced out of the bank and Claire saw to her horror that one of them carried a gun. Jane had rushed over to her brother and she and several passers-by helped him to sit up. Someone was screaming as the two men made a dash for the car. A man in the crowd threw himself after the third raider and brought him to the ground with a flying tackle. As they struggled, the second man turned and fired in their direction. Fortunately the bullet missed, struck the pavement and ricocheted straight through the window of the bank leaving a small neat hole. By this time Claire had rushed to join Jane where Philip was struggling to his feet. He had a nasty graze along his forehead and a bump was already forming but apart from that, he seemed unhurt.

Inside the bank a loud alarm was sounding and a large crowd was gathering. The third raider still wrestled with his attacker and finally threw him to the ground and ran after the white car which was already moving away. It seemed to Claire that everything happened in slow motion and yet in fact it was all over in a matter of seconds.

(From *The Willerbys and the Bank Robbers* by Pamela Oldfield.)

1 Give the passage a title.
2 When one of the robbers fired a gun the bullet *ricocheted*.
    Read this part of the passage carefully for clues to the meaning of 'ricocheted'. Write down what you think it means, and then use a dictionary to see if you were right.
3 Pretend you are Philip. Describe what happened to you.
4 Now pretend you are one of the passers-by. Describe what you saw.
5 A passer-by tried to stop one of the robbers. Do you think this was a sensible thing to do? Give a reason for your answer.
6 Study the picture for two minutes. Then turn to the bottom of page 59 and answer the questions there without looking back.

To talk about
1 What would you have done if you had seen the bank robbery?
2 What questions do you think the police would ask the passers-by?
3 Have you ever witnessed a robbery or an accident? Tell the class what happened. Include as much detail as you can.

Reading for clues

Think for yourself what the missing words are in this passage.
Write one word for each space.

> 'Are you all right, Philip?' she asked.
>
> He ___1___ dazedly and everyone around them started talking at once. ___2___ shouted for the police and several of the bank ___3___ ran out on to the pavement to stare after ___4___ disappearing car.
>
> 'I knew we would be next! I ___5___ knew it!'
>
> They turned to see a large, elderly ___6___ standing on the top step.
>
> A woman beside Claire ___7___, 'That's Mr Humphrey, the manager.'
>
> Someone else said, 'I ___8___ how much they've taken?'
>
> 'I hope no-one's hurt.'
>
> 'How ___9___ they get away with it?'
>
> The knee of Philip's ___10___ was torn and Claire noticed that his knee was ___11___ to bleed.
>
> (From *The Willerbys and the Bank Robbers* by Pamela Oldfield.)

Map squares

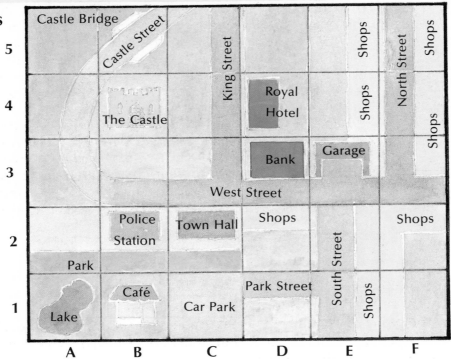

Look at this map. The squares you can see are called grid squares. They are useful to help you to find things on the map.

Look for the castle. Its grid square is in column **B** and row **4**. We say that the castle is in square **B4**.

1 What is in each of these grid squares?
   B1, D3, E3, C2, F3?
2 Write the grid square for the lake, the Police Station, the car park and the Royal Hotel.
3 Look carefully at the map. Write *True, False* or *Can't Say* for each of these statements:
   a) There is a bridge in grid square **B5**.
   b) The Royal Hotel is on West Street.
   c) The café is very busy.
   d) There are no shops near the castle.
   e) The garage is on West Street.
   f) The Town Hall is opposite the bank.

Robbery

	Details	Clues
Date:	June 20th	The calendar shows it.
Time of robbery:		
Thief entered by:		
Thief left by:		
Stolen articles:		
Injury to owner:		
Weapon used:		

1 Copy the heading from the detective's notebook. Look closely at the picture and fill in the details.
2 What other clues might you look for?
3 Pretend you are the owner of the jewels. Write an account of what happened to you.

Suspects

Detective Inspector Clewson has four suspects. He hurries back to the police station to compare the fingerprints on the jewellery box with those of his four suspects.

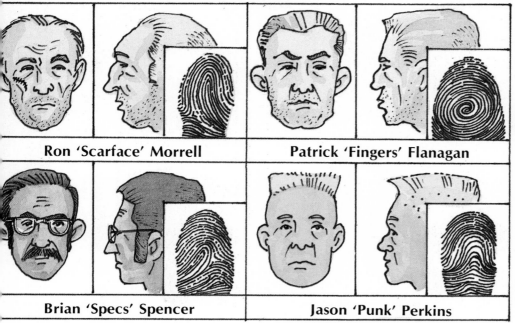

Ron 'Scarface' Morrell

Patrick 'Fingers' Flanagan

Brian 'Specs' Spencer

Jason 'Punk' Perkins

1 Who is the thief? How do you know?
2 Make up a *Wanted* poster for him, like this one.

WANTED
CHARLIE ARLEY
RED HAIR
FLAT NOSE
BLUE EYES
SCAR ON LEFT CHEEK
FOR ARMED ROBBERY
£100 REWARD FOR INFORMATION LEADING TO HIS CAPTURE

3 When Inspector Clewson catches him, the thief writes a full confession of the crime. He tells how he broke into the house, how he found the jewels, and how he struck the owner of the house with a poker before escaping. Pretend you are the thief. Write his full confession.

Activities

1 Make up a *Wanted* poster for a classmate. Look closely at the shape of his face, his nose, eyes, ears and mouth. Draw or paint his picture, and then add a description of him. Invent an amusing 'crime' for him and offer a reward.

2 Ask a friend to 'steal' an object from the room. Watch him carefully and then write a full description of what you see.
Your account should include:
— a description of the thief
— where he went
— how he moved
— a description of the object stolen
— anything else you saw or heard which would help the police.

Looking and remembering

When you have looked carefully at the picture on page 56, answer these questions. Do not look back at the picture.

1 What time did the robbery take place?
2 What was the colour and registration of the car?
3 Was the gunman right-handed or left-handed?
4 Write a description of each of the robbers.

UNIT 15   Storm

What a night it was! The salty wind was going round and round in circles, first whipping them forward, then holding them up, then barging them towards the hedge on one side of the lane or the deep ditch on the other. The horseman kept one arm round Annie and Annie held onto the horse. The rain flew straight at them, spiteful drops sharp as pins and needles.

Then Annie began to sway in the saddle. She thought she could bear it no longer — the furious gallop, the gallop of the storm, the storm of her own fears. What can I do? What if I never get to Doctor Grant?

But the horseman only shouted and spurred his horse to go even faster. He seemed bent on going where he was going as quickly as he possibly could. Faster and faster! So that when Annie looked about her again, there she was! There she was in sleeping Waterslain. The chestnut mare was sweating and blowing out big puffs of condensed air.

'Down Staithe Street,' gasped Annie. 'Doctor Grant.'

The horseman galloped straight up the middle of the village street. The horse's hooves clattered on the tarmac and Annie saw that several times they struck sparks from pieces of chert and flint. Then they turned into Staithe Street and 'Whoa!' shouted the horseman in his dark voice.

'Whoa!' And his mare at last slowed down to a trot.

'There!' said Annie, pointing to a gateway flanked by laurel bushes. 'We're there!'

Doctor Grant's lights were still on. His curtains were the colour of ripe peaches. And a lantern, swaying in his porch, threw a pool of soft shifting light over the flagstones and gravel outside the front door.

(From *Storm* by Kevin Crossley-Holland.)

1   Why do you think they were out riding on such a wild night?
2   What was dangerous about the wind?
3   Why do you think the author says 'the gallop of the storm'?
4   What was Annie most afraid of?
5   Which words in the last paragraph tell us they were arriving very late in the evening?

Reading for clues

Think for yourself what the missing words are in this passage.
Write one word for each space.

> Annie stared and stared as if she had ____1____ seen bright light before.
> In the gloom of the ____2____ storm, nothing had looked quite definite
> and many things ____3____ frightening: the reaching arms of the tree, the
> fallen body ____4____ the milk churn, the gleam and flash of water.
> ____5____ was the danger, too, of meeting these chancy things ____6____
> only come out at night — will-o'-the-wykes and bogles and boggarts
> ____7____ the black dog, Shuck . . . and worst of all there ____8____ the
> ghost. But now, in the clear light, there was ____9____ longer room for
> anything uncertain or ghostly.
>
> (From *Storm* by Kevin Crossley-Holland.)

To talk about

1 Did you like the story? Give a reason for your answer.
2 The author tells us that the raindrops were as sharp as pins and needles. Can you think of words to describe how these things feel:
   a) drizzle
   b) hailstones
   c) a cold winter's wind
   d) the sun in mid-summer
   e) an icicle?
3 Describe the worst weather you can remember. Try to make the class feel how horrible it was.
4 In what ways can bad weather be dangerous? Think of storms, blizzards and fog. Which people have to work even in the worst of weathers?
5 Are you afraid of thunder and lightning? Can you say why? What do you do when there is a thunderstorm? Why should you never shelter under a tree during a thunderstorm?

Writing

Look at the picture. Imagine you are out in this storm on a dark night. Write a description, or a poem, about what you see and hear. Don't forget to describe the wind and the rain, and what it feels like as you get wetter and wetter.

Reading

Look for the book *Storm* by Kevin Crossley-Holland in your library or bookshop, and read more about Annie and the mysterious horseman.

From **A Song of Wind**
Hark to the song of the scattering, scurrying,
Blustering, bullying, bellowing, hurrying
    Wind!
Over the hills it comes, laughing and rollicking,
Curling and whirling, flying and frolicking,
    Spinning the clouds that are scattered and thinned.
        And shouting a song
        As it gallops along
    A song that is nothing but wind.
Will Lawson

1 Can you think of any other action words
   which tell how the wind moves and
   sounds? Make a list.
2 Write a similar poem about the rain.
   Here are some words to start you off.

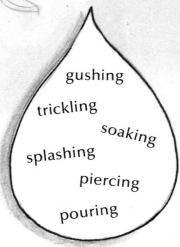

gushing

trickling

soaking

splashing

piercing

pouring

Television weather symbols

Sleet

Dull weather cloud
Thunderstorm
Snow
Sunshine
Fairweather cloud
Temperature in degrees
Sunny intervals
Rain
Wind speed and direction
Sleet
Rain showers and sunny intervals

Here are some of the symbols you have seen on television weather forecasts. Copy them into
your book and match each one with its meaning. The first one has been done for you.

The Beaufort Scale

Force	Wind	Speed (miles per hour)	Effect
0	Calm	1	Smoke rises straight up.
1	Light air	1-3	Smoke drifts slightly.
2	Light breeze	4-7	Leaves rustle, wind felt on face.
3	Gentle breeze	8-12	Leaves move on trees.
4	Moderate breeze	13-18	Loose paper blows, small branches move.
5	Fresh breeze	19-24	Small trees move.
6	Strong breeze	25-31	Large branches sway, telephone wires whistle.
7	Moderate gale	32-38	Whole trees sway, difficult to walk against the wind.
8	Fresh gale	39-46	Twigs break off trees, very hard to walk against the wind.
9	Strong gale	47-54	Chimney pots blow off, large branches break off.
10	Whole gale	55-63	Trees uprooted, serious damage to buildings.
11	Storm	64-72	Houses badly damaged.
12	Hurricane	72+	Disaster, whole area laid waste.

The Beaufort Scale shows thirteen different strengths of wind from 0 (Calm) to 12 (Hurricane). Look carefully at the chart and the six pictures above. What force of wind does each picture show? The first one has been done for you.

A	Force 0

Now do these.

1 How fast is the wind at force 11?
2 How fast is the wind at force 8?
3 What is the speed and force of a hurricane?
4 What happens in a fresh breeze?
5 What happens in a strong gale?
6 What happens in a light breeze?

Writing
Imagine you set off on a journey on a sunny day when the wind is force 0. Use the chart above to help you describe what happens as the wind slowly increases to force 10.

Make-a-story chart

Start at the STORM box. Follow an arrow to another box, and so on. You should now have some ideas for an exciting story.

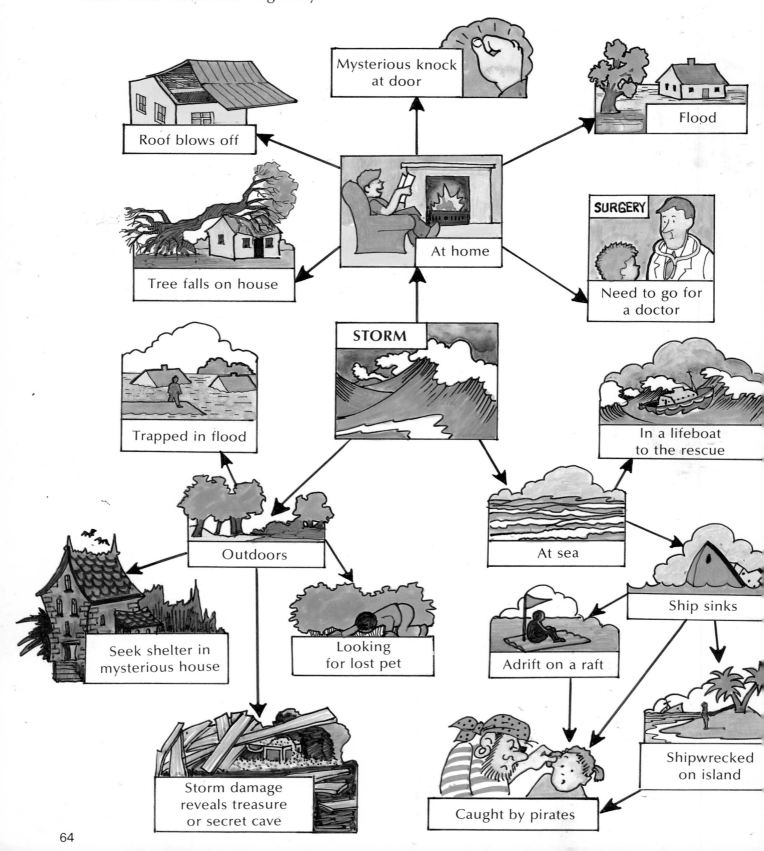

Roof blows off

Mysterious knock at door

Flood

Tree falls on house

At home

SURGERY

Need to go for a doctor

Trapped in flood

STORM

In a lifeboat to the rescue

Outdoors

At sea

Ship sinks

Seek shelter in mysterious house

Looking for lost pet

Adrift on a raft

Shipwrecked on island

Storm damage reveals treasure or secret cave

Caught by pirates